FREEDOM,
AUTHORITY, AND
THE YOUNG ADULT

FREEDOM, AUTHORITY, AND THE YOUNG ADULT

A Report to the Department of Education and Science on the Young Adult Resource Project; in particular examining how the resources of adults are used by young people as they take up full adult roles in society.

by

JOHN BAZALGETTE MA DipEd

PITMAN PUBLISHING

First published 1971
Reprinted 1972

Sir Isaac Pitman and Sons Ltd
Pitman House, Parker Street, Kingsway, London WC2B 5PB
PO Box 46038, Portal Street, Nairobi, Kenya

Sir Isaac Pitman (Aust) Pty Ltd
Pitman House, 158 Bouverie Street, Carlton, Victoria 3053, Australia

Pitman Publishing Company SA Ltd
PO Box 11231, Johannesburg, South Africa

Pitman Publishing Corporation
6 East 43rd Street, New York, NY 10017, USA

Sir Isaac Pitman (Canada) Ltd
495 Wellington Street West, Toronto 135, Canada

The Copp Clark Publishing Company
517 Wellington Street West, Toronto 135, Canada

ISBN: 0 273 36145 7

Reproduced and printed by photolithography and bound in
Great Britain at The Pitman Press, Bath

G2—(G.4663:15)

Acknowledgments

The Young Adult Resource Project, and its report, could not have been completed without the guidance and help of a great many people. It began from Bruce Reed's original ideas about young people and as things have developed other people have been drawn in. It is essentially the result of their co-operation, not of one individual's efforts. In the first place I have been supported and encouraged throughout the four years by the Project Steering Committee:

> Professor J W Tibble (Chairman)
> Mr J H Fitch
> Mr F D Flower
> Mrs E Hoodless
> Rev B D Reed
> Miss J E Richardson
> Mr R G Tweed
>
> Miss N Newton-Smith (HMI Observer)

On many occasions, especially during the first two years of the Project, they have found it difficult to know where things were going. Yet they have always been generous in giving me time to see them whenever I wanted their advice on specific issues. They have also read and commented on the drafts of the reports I have produced during the four years, including this one. I would especially like to thank John Fitch and Fred Flower for their help with early versions of this final document.

The Department of Education and Science, on the advice of the Youth Service Development Council, the Christian Teamwork Trust, the Elizabeth Whitelaw Reid Club and the Grubb Institute have between them provided the finance which has enabled the Project to be carried out. In particular it was the award of a grant by the Department which gave us the opportunity to go ahead in the first place.

I am glad to acknowledge my gratitude to the many bodies who have helped carry out this study by letting me work with the young people for whom they have been responsible: Archway School, Bishop Giffard School, Essex Flour and Grain Co Ltd, EWR Club, Inner London Probation and After-care

Service, the Borough of Islington Children's Department, Islington Green School, Kingsway College for Further Education, the Lyndhurst Club, Metcalfe, Cooper and Hepburn Ltd, Rubery Owen and Co Ltd, and St William of York School.

These bodies have introduced me to the 300 young adults without whose help and cooperation this study could not have been carried out. It has been the willingness of these young adults to be associated with me, formally and informally, through membership of a small working group or as a result of our having met at the EWR or Lyndhurst Clubs, which has been essential to my being able to do any work at all. Some of them I am glad to be able to continue to meet as personal friends.

I have also received the help of over 80 adults who have been prepared to visit the groups of young people, talking with them about their own work. They have known that they were taking part in a research project and that I was studying how they behaved in relation to the young people they met. I am indebted to them because between them they have enabled me to identify many of the important factors in the relationship between adults and young people.

Finally, I am happy to record my debt to my colleagues at the Grubb Institute: to Bruce Reed from whose original ideas this project sprang, and who has always taken my understanding of what I was involved in further and deeper than I could ever have done on my own; to Barry Palmer who has helped me find ways of expressing things more clearly and concisely; to Mary Reed for her wise advice about the way young adults feel and think about life; and to Jean Hutton and Helen Woodhead who have guided the team of secretaries, Jane Clitheroe, Denise Moll, Penny Mountjoy, Diana Neal and Marion Turbard who have done the typing and duplicating involved in producing the reports arising from the project including this one. As my colleagues will all know, the ideas expressed and developed in this report are not the product of any one person, but are the result of discussion and comparison of what we have all been doing and thinking in our different fields of work. Nevertheless the way the ideas are expressed in this report is my responsibility alone and my colleagues are not bound to agree with what I have said or how I have said it.

J. L. B.
August 1970

Contents

1. The Problem

THE BACKGROUND

1966 was a peaceful year as far as the Press reporting on the activities of
young people was concerned. The high tide of violence by 'mods' and 'rockers'
on the beaches of Brighton, Southend and other seaside resorts had receded.
Books had appeared which helped to keep the issue alive as a subject likely to
arouse strong emotions. Anyone who wished to engage in a discussion about
the behaviour of young people could be provided with the feeling that they spoke
with authority if they had read such books as 'Generation X' or 'Teenage
Revolution', 'Absolute Beginners' or even the now classic 'Roaring Boys'. [1]

At that point there was a sense that what society was up against was its
failure to provide satisfactory educational opportunities for people from working class backgrounds, a failure which was seen to result in violence and
delinquency. There was widespread belief that Mr Crosland's influential
Circular 10/65, requesting plans from all education authorities for a reorgan-
isation of secondary schools on comprehensive lines, linked with the commitment to raise the school leaving age to 16 in 1970, together marked the
beginning of the end of facing the consequences of this failure. Nevertheless
at the same time as hopes were rising about that state of affairs there were
signs that a new phenomenon was beginning to appear. The figures for drug
taking, especially the Home Office figures of young people addicted to heroin,
were increasing at an alarming rate, added to which the circulation of am-
phetamines such as 'Purple Hearts' was becoming almost commonplace in
certain parts of London. During the summer of 1966 a growing number of
young people, many from middle class backgrounds, could be found simply
drifting around London, homeless and jobless. It took a further eighteen
months or so before the 'hippies' began to make themselves seriously felt.
Coinciding with them was the rise of 'student militancy'. As far as the news
media were concerned a high point for this movement was reached with the
storming of the American Embassy in Grosvenor Square in March 1968.

1967 and 1968 saw the first 'sit-ins' at the London School of Economics,

1

Hornsey College of Art and other colleges and universities. The summer of 1969 saw the swelling of the permanent population of Piccadilly Circus and nearby Green Park which overflowed into the occupation of 144 Piccadilly, initially as a protest on behalf of the homeless but which soon became a symbol of a number of other things, one of which was the revolt of young people against the society in which they found themselves. They left behind them the inscription which until the autumn of 1970 warned those who passed: 'We are the writing on your wall'. At this point the 'skinheads' appeared. From the attention given them by the Press and TV it seemed that society would rather return to coping with the threat posed by 'disadvantaged' working class boys, than the 'advantaged' middle class.

On Thursday, 21 March 1968, a few days after the Grosvenor Square demonstration, a letter was published in 'The Times'. It was from Mr Peter Cadogan, Secretary of the Committee of 100, who had been present in the Square. He wrote:

> "What happened on March 17 was not a transient phenomenon. The demonstrators, average age, about 19, will learn from their mistakes. They will not give up, they will not be preached at from anyone's pulpit or armchair and they will not be deterred by penalties. March 17 showed that there is hope for England yet. We have at last located a backbone. The most alarming thing is the incomprehension of the parents' generation. They do not know, and do not seem to want to know what their sons and daughters are up to. Are older people incapable of anger and action against inhumanity?
> Yours truly, Peter Cadogan"

Though it followed one particular incident, this letter contained remarks which could have been made pertinently by articulate young people at any time in the late 1960s. It draws attention to the nature of the relationship felt to exist between adults and young people and particularly the feelings which this arouses in the young.

THE PROJECT OUTLINED

It was against this kind of developing background that the Young Adult Resource Project was started. Following work which had been done amongst young people by Christian Teamwork (now the Grubb Institute of Behavioural Studies), the Youth Service Development Council advised the Department of Education and Science to award the Institute a three-year grant to investigate the issues involved in helping adolescents make the transition to taking a full adult role in society. The Project was to begin by establishing work in connection with the Elizabeth Whitelaw Reid Club in Islington, North London, a club already sponsored by Christian Teamwork and working along lines pioneered since 1958 by the Lyndhurst Club in Kentish Town, under the same sponsorship.

The original application for a grant suggested that the problems experienced by young people in taking up adult roles concerned understanding the nature and use of authority. This was seen to involve two related processes:

i.   To recognise and respond constructively to external authority as it is
represented by those who may be seen as leaders in society, such as
employers, magistrates, clergymen, as well as parents. This response
includes learning to work at the problems of bringing about change,
which **may** bring people into conflict with those in designated positions
of authority.

ii. To understand how to accept responsibility for one's own actions, that
is to recognise one's own authority in the different roles one takes. A
special feature of the Project was to be to understand the contribution
which can be made to these two processes by the churches.

In one way the Project could be defined as an investigation into the nature
of the leadership required to help these two processes to take place together
and thus help young people take up full adult roles in society. More particularly the Project came to focus on studying the conditions under which young
people are able to make use of the resources of adults to help them grow up,
and the conditions under which they are inhibited from using such resources.
Four working hypotheses were outlined which led to the construction of the
kind of models which enabled the detailed examination of the problem. This
meant that the hypotheses might be modified, added to and changed, as work
developed in taking the investigation forward.   They are stated here in the form
in which they were originally set out in 1966 at the beginning of the Project.

These were the working hypotheses:

1.   The problem of the use of authority is the central problem of young
people between the ages of 15 and 21.

2.   In order to understand the nature of authority it is necessary to recognise the structures of society, roles, boundaries and resources. For
young adults this can be done in the first place in structures such as
those at work or at school rather than in the family.

3.   The resource persons most useful to young people in their development
are those who are aware of their own roles in the authority structure
of society and are also able to take this into account in their relationships with young people.

4.   To enable young people to explore the use of authority it is necessary
to find or create situations where they can learn from their experience
of relationships with those in authority.

NOTES

(1) C Hamblett and   Generation X   Sphere Books 1964
     J Deverson

     Peter Laurie   Teenage Revolution   Blond 1965

     Colin McInnes   Absolute Beginners   Penguin 1964

     Edward Blishen   Roaring Boys   Panther 1966

2. The Search for a Method

At the outset of the Project it was unclear what kind of method would be appropriate. One thing which seemed to be necessary was that I, as the Project Officer, should find ways of involving myself in the lives of a number of young people so that it would be possible to be with them as they made the transition to full adulthood. This inevitably had the disadvantage that to become too close to anyone over a period of years would be likely to make objective study of the process exceedingly difficult and probably impossible. The problem would be to identify sufficiently my own contributions, both good and bad, and describe them in a way which would enable other people to learn from them.   More especially I felt that what emerged must enable new ideas and approaches to be developed from it; a report which simply recounted the activities of one adult with a number of young people would be most unlikely to help with that. It was obvious therefore that something else had to be found.

At the time I began to work on the Project there was a trend of new work with young people already established. Mary Morse had published her report of work done through the National Association of Youth Clubs [1] with young people who were not attached to any recognised Youth Organisation; George Goetschius and Joan Tash were on the point of publishing the report of their work with similar people, done in conjunction with the Young Women's Christian Association. [2]   Both these projects had been assisted by grants given on the advice of the Youth Service Development Council. Such projects as these, and there were a growing number of them in the country, aimed at developing continuing relationships with young people in informal situations and living through an extended period of time with them. They were mainly projects which had a team of workers and a supervisor, with the latter responsible for the development of the project and its writing up.   The basic approach, that of contacting young people informally in the streets, cafes and pubs, was already decided and studies were made of how this approach was used and what problems they encountered.

At about the same time other important pieces of work were appearing

4

which concerned the development of young people. The work of the Eppels on the morality of adolescents, [3] Michael Schofield on sexual behaviour, [4] David Downes' study of delinquency in East London[5] and Peter Willmott's book on adolescent boys in the same area, [6] were either published or on the horizon in 1966. These studies were of a mainly sociological type involving questionnaires and interviews.

There were also a large number of more personal accounts of work with young people, many of them were published as articles in journals such as 'New Society', 'Youth Review' and 'Prospect'. George Burton's book on his work at the Mayflower Family Centre in Canning Town was an outstanding example of this kind of work, [7] particularly because of the description of his integration of his Christian faith with his work with the young people of the area.

Each of these pieces of work is important and they make different contributions to understanding aspects of work with young adults, but each takes different things for granted and leaves them largely unexplored. None of them fully illuminates the problems of the use of authority encountered by young people, nor do they enable an extensive analysis of how the resources of adults are used or perceived by young people. The different methods they adopted did not seem directly useful to the Project which I was undertaking.

In the opening months I began to work on three fronts: I spent time in the streets around Islington trying to contact young people who might be regarded as 'unattached' in the Youth Service sense of the term; I also worked with the team of Christian adults who were endeavouring to re-open the Elizabeth Whitelaw Reid Club (EWR) and for two days a month I went to the Education Department of a large engineering firm in the Midlands and worked with apprentices and young trainees as part of their own developing work. After about five months the work in the Midlands was drawn to a close, mainly because some of the important things which began to emerge were clearly suitable to be transferred to the situation in Islington.

It also soon became apparent that the casual contacts made with young people in streets and public places in Islington were likely to prove largely fruitless even for finding new members of the EWR Club. It appeared that I threatened young people as I met them. In order to overcome the fear I engendered it would have been necessary to have denied or deliberately distorted parts of the truth about myself. This was not an experience which was unique to me; it had been reported by the majority of those who had carried out work in this fashion. [1, 2] Alternatively, I could have invested a long time in making the initial contacts. This did not seem to be appropriate because of the urgency of the problem. To overcome the fear, to avoid telling lies about myself and to make the maximum use of time, it seemed necessary to construct other situations within which to work, situations in which young people would have

5

freedom to make use of whatever resources I might have to offer them, and also have freedom to reject those resources if they felt they were inappropriate. Alongside giving freedom to accept or reject those resources, there was also the necessity to help young people to assess realistically the nature of the resources and their relevance to problems accepted as being relevant to young adults.

Comparing the responses of the young men at the engineering firm with those met casually in Islington, it was obvious that the most creative opportunities occurred where real conflict, tension or stress were able to be identified, expressed and worked through. The conflict might be about the nature of the problem, the relevance of the resources available or the way I offered those resources. Such opportunities had appeared on a number of occasions with the young employees meeting at their place of work, but had never occurred at all in the streets and cafes. On the few occasions in which conflict or stress had been likely to arise, young people would either withdraw completely by walking off or would effectively flee by turning to operate a juke box, pin table, or one-armed bandit if such things were about. What was evident from this was that work needed to be concentrated through the structures to which young people were in fact attached, and from which they derived at least some sense of security.

In the first place the opening of the EWR Club provided one such structure and so concentrated work began there. In addition, approaches were made to schools and employers to try to find ways of working with young people belonging to other structures.

The EWR Club is structured in such a way as to enable the young people who join it to experience the problems of authority involved in running the Club and share this experience with the adult team. The Club's day-to-day affairs are in the hands of the Members' Committee on which both the team and the members are represented, with the adults always in the minority. The Members' Chairman is the focus of the authority structure of the Club: this role is never taken by an adult team member. A further significant feature of the structure is the fact that the adult team have another role and also constitute the Management Committee of the Club.

What was quickly apparent was that it was now possible for me both to develop relationships with young people myself and also observe something of how other adults did the same ; it was also possible to see that young people were learning a number of things about authority and the problems of being an adult. It was, however, far too diverse and complex a situation to carry out a real study of how the resources of adults were being offered and used. This made the development of another method imperative.

Early in 1967 two schools and one firm gave me the chance to work with young people for whom they were responsible. This led to the development of

the small working group method which has been the main tool used in the
Project. The task of the group has been the same as that of the EWR and
Lyndhurst Clubs, being to provide a framework within which adults and young
people can meet and develop an understanding of each other through exploring
together the nature and use of authority in the situation in which they find
themselves. The difference lies in the size of the model being used, the working groups had 5-12 young people, myself as Project Officer and one visiting
adult, whereas the EWR Club has up to 130 members, up to 20 members of
the team and a variety of different kinds of visiting adults. The small working
group thus provided a controlled situation in which aspects of the behaviour
of adults and young people could be studied.

Since the Project began, 14 different groups have been taken. These have
been drawn from the following settings:

Schools	6
Further Education	2
Employment	3
Probation	1
Child Care	1
Youth Club	1

The school groups have been drawn from four different schools, three
comprehensive and one secondary modern; the two groups from further education were drawn from Kingsway College for Further Education, both groups
being on day release from the Civil Service, the GPO and large commercial
institutions; the groups from employment were two groups of van boys and a
group of printing apprentices. In the group drawn from the Inner London Probation and After-Care Service some members were first offenders and some
had previous convictions; the least skilled was a van boy and most skilled a
trainee soil chemist. The Children's Department group was made up of young
people mainly in family situations. The youth club group were all members
of the EWR Club. Groups have varied in size from 5-14, the majority being
around 10-11 members.

The range of young people with whom work has been done has been very
wide. They have been aged between 14 and 21 years old, each group usually
having an age span of about 18 months between the oldest and the youngest,
except in the case of school groups where the range was narrower.   In the
first year it was easy to have access to the academically and socially inadequate, the second year provided opportunities for involving those from more
stable social and employment backgrounds. In the final year work was done
with some who subsequently entered university as well as some who finished
up in borstal. Generalisations made from this experience therefore seem to
have relevance to all young adults in their relations with those who offer resources to them.

7

THE SMALL WORKING GROUP METHOD

The primary task of each small working group used in the Project has been **to provide opportunities for its members to meet adults and explore with them problems arising from the nature and use of authority.**

Each group met for a series of weekly meetings lasting one and a half hours, spread over periods between three and six months and which went through three phases. In the first phase, which lasted 2-3 sessions, the members of the group met with me alone and discussed with me their previous experiences of how authority had been exercised. Discussion ranged around their experiences at school, relations with their teachers or the problems of having been prefects, their relations with employers, the police and others in society. At this stage I worked in such a way as to try to demonstrate that I had skills and experience which I offered to the group for use on their own terms, which might include their rejecting my resources. During this phase, part of the work arose from examination of different experiences of leadership members had met, including looking at the way I took my own role in the group they were attending. The purpose of the first phase was to introduce the group to ways of looking at problems of authority which they had opportunities of testing out in later meetings.

Example I

It may be helpful to pause a moment and describe one such session in order to illustrate this point in the life of a group. In this instance I was meeting a group of eight young employees from a printing firm. Some of them were apprentices but two worked in the offices as clerks and one was from the warehouse. They had received a brief written description of the work of the group and had then chosen to come to the meetings. They came with the permission of their overseers and managers since the sessions took place during working hours on the firm's premises. I introduced the series, talking about the group meetings providing opportunities to learn about authority and to meet different people whose job entailed exercising authority. The discussion of what we would do was slow and rather desultory until one boy said 'I suppose it's going to be just like liberal studies at college'. I immediately took this up saying that I did not know about liberal studies at college but we were meeting on their firm's premises, in the firm's time, and my understanding of my own authority in the situation was that I had to do my best to make what happened in this group relate in some way to what their company existed to do. After a moment of silence the atmosphere changed and a lively discussion ensued of the work of trades unions, their own position in them and how trades unionism related to the overall part of the company. I was able to offer ways of looking at the problems they raised, drawing diagrams to help illustrate different points, and showing some of the differences in the authority of a manager of the company and that of a trades unionist.

In this session it was possible for the group to identify what we had met to explore, some of the ideas we would be using were introduced and the members were able to see that the kind of relationship they would establish with me would be different from the conventional teacher/student one they had anticipated. It is worth adding that not all such first sessions were as quick to recognise the need to work in this way; some took three sessions or even more to reach a comparable stage. Nevertheless this session does illustrate how a number of introductory sessions developed.

The second phase entailed visitors coming to the group representing different institutions in society and having different experiences of the exercise of authority. These visitors were drawn from a list compiled by the group itself during an early session, and they came in to discuss their role in society with the young adults. Visitors were seen by me as resources to be used in the group to help carry out its task.

At this stage there were opportunities for the members to examine the visitor's past experience of exercising authority, to study his or her response to the young people within the group and their responses to him, and to use their own experience to help them explore and test the visitor's statements. Clearly, all the members did not do this all the time but it was evident that many of them took these opportunities at various times during a series. During these meetings I worked in such a way as to help the group – by asking questions that opened up relevant areas for exploration – by making interpretations to help understand the relationship which developed between the visitor and myself and the group – and by referring to previous incidents in the group's life.

At this stage there was a great deal of variety in the way groups behaved. In order to illustrate some of this I offer four examples, each of which conveys a different atmosphere and behaviour.

Example II

The five boys in the group were all on probation. The group had met about ten times before and the last visitor, a hospital ward sister, was present. The setting was a basement lounge at the probation offices, with large, rather overwhelming leather chairs, a musty smell and the walls painted a penetrating shade of yellow.

The hospital sister was in her mid-twenties, small and attractive. She was the first woman to visit the group. The boys, aged between 15 and 18, were impressed by her femininity and from the first set out to gain her attention one way or another. Jimmy, a rather inarticulate redhead, got noisier and more obscene in his allusions; Frank sniggered and made gestures at Jimmy, whereas Chris was excessively sane and reasonable, asking serious

9

questions about delays in getting treated in hospitals, the problems about privacy in the wards and so on. He turned on Jimmy at one stage for being obscene, though he quite clearly took some pleasure from what had been said. What clearly concerned them all from the beginning was the question of sexuality and how to cope with it in this session. After accusing all doctors of being 'randy brutes' Chris asked the nurse, 'Are nurses virgins?' to which she replied, 'Some are and some are not, like all women'. I pointed out to them that they were having difficulty in separating the visitor's womanhood from her role as a nurse.

From this the discussion was led round to an open exploration of sexuality and the boys' problems surrounding their own feelings about women. Frequently the boys had not got the appropriate language to express what they were trying to get at and at one stage when asking a question about male virility all Jimmy could do was to gesticulate graphically and grunt to make his point. The nurse took his questions quite straight and replied 'I think it would be unlikely for a man to be able to do that'. Immediately after this remark Chris looked round at everyone, including myself, and said, 'You know, she's the only person in the room who isn't blushing'.

Example III

There were fourteen boys present from the school, a boys' school in North London. They were meeting in a room in a youth club during school hours. The visitor was a probation officer and he was the first person to visit the group. He introduced himself very briefly and described his job as being 'to make personal relationships with people in trouble and by so doing to help them by giving them a chance to explore their problems'. At first the boys were interested and attentive to what he had to say, but they found the answers to their questions to be too enigmatic for them to understand. The probation officer did not seem to give a straight answer, but seemed to twist it in such a way as to make it appear to question the boys rather than to answer them. They began to feel themselves to be under attack and started to fall silent leaving the questioning to be carried on by the only coloured boy in the group.

I could feel tension and anger rising, both in the group and in myself. As the boys became more and more conscious of this tension, they began to leave the room, ostensibly to go to the lavatory, but soon only six of them were left. Their absence began to weigh on the group, silences became longer, the probation officer began to be more and more agitated and at times even ignored the occasional question addressed to him. He demonstrated in his behaviour that whatever he said his job was about in the opening minutes of the session, what he actually did in the group militated against his achieving it.

As the session developed I felt myself more and more under pressure

10

to defend the visitor and I found that as I contributed to what little discussion there was, my remarks were coming across in an increasingly aggressive way. As this happened the feelings of fear and anxiety in all of us were further heightened. I was conscious that any differences between my role in the group and that of the visitor were rapidly being obscured and we were being seen as two adults behaving in a punitive and unhelpful way. I felt frustrated and hurt, not only by the boys but also by the probation officer, because I had been so inadequate in the situation. When the session was over, I found that the boys who had left the room had stolen a packet of cigarettes and a box of matches from the pocket of an old age pensioner's coat which had been hanging downstairs.

Example IV

Eight out of ten day-release students, young men and women, were present when a headmaster visited a group in further education. They were almost all junior civil servants, coming from grammar school backgrounds, most of them having done at least part of a sixth form course. The visitor was the headmaster of a large comprehensive school which is working at the problems of being progressive in a very depressed area in London.

The headmaster conveyed the picture of a person who was interested in his pupils, was concerned to have a good school, offering different kinds of opportunities of broadening their horizons through outings and foreign visits and similar things. He talked at length about how records on pupils were kept, school uniform, school dances, his open office which was frequented by sixth formers dropping in for a chat during lunch hours and appeared as an excellent salesman for his school. He succeeded in making the members of the group jealous of the fact that they had not been to his school. By doing this he robbed them of their capacity to look critically at what he had to say, and of drawing on their own experience of schools to help them to do this.

I drew attention to what I believed he was doing to them, adding that their own head teachers would probably paint a similar picture of their own schools if they gave them the opportunity they were giving this visitor. Work as I would, I could not break the mutual seduction which went on. The headmaster talked for longer and longer, the group's questions were more and more designed to keep him talking as they listened, spellbound. The bell for the end of the session went, I thanked him for coming, got up and switched off the tape recorder, but still he went on talking and they went on listening. Five minutes elapsed between the bell sounding and my switching off the tape, but he was still going strong at that moment. I have no record of how much longer he talked, but it was not until after I had packed up the machine that he finally stopped.

11

Example V

There were ten boys present, all van boys from the same firm and a Police Inspector in uniform was the visitor. The boys were aged between 15 and 17, mostly being nearer 15. The Inspector tipped his chair back, smacked his gloves into his hand and said, 'So you don't like the police, eh?'.

For the next ten minutes all bedlam was let loose. The boys claimed to have had many experiences with the police. They had been roughly handled, a mate had been 'done over' in a cell, the police were all 'bent' and so on. They were angry and wanted a reply. To most of what they had said the officer replied in a way which seemed almost calculated to keep the fight going, but the main gist of which was that he had never known 'that sort of thing' to happen in his time.

Then suddenly a change came over the boys. They seemed to realise that they would get little satisfaction from the line of enquiry they were pursuing and they began to ask questions about arming the police, bringing back hanging. 'What do you think about Harry Roberts who shot those coppers up in Shepherds Bush?' and similar questions. For a few moments the policeman tried to keep the fight going, but the pressure from the boys was too strong so he followed the lead they were giving and answered their questions on the basis of the facts of his experience. Though the group met after work before they had a chance to go home for their supper, the session went on for half an hour longer than normal.

The final stage, lasting 2-3 sessions, provided opportunities for myself and the group to review the whole experience and to come to some conclusions about it. This included trying to see how some of that experience could be applied to other parts of the group members' lives.

These sessions were always the most difficult. The conversation was slow, there were many periods of silence. At times I felt that I wanted to talk a lot to cover up the problem of ending and at other times I felt angry that members appeared so inept at reflecting on what had happened either in the group or elsewhere in their lives. When it came to the time to end, people often hung around trying to find a way of continuing the session or planning to meet again sometime in the future. I usually found it very difficult to get my things together for myself, and to leave without seeming to make unnecessary fuss or being standoffish.

ROLES TAKEN IN THE GROUPS

The word 'role' appears frequently in current sociological and social psychological discussion, with a number of different shades of meaning. Where the precise meaning is not clarified, confusion inevitably results. In the context of this report I propose to use the term 'role' to mean that pattern of activities or behaviour which contributes to the carrying out of the task or aspect of the task of a group.

As I came to recognise the different roles in the structure of the groups and their importance in the way they affected people's behaviour, I found ways of helping groups to explore other differences in a constructive fashion especially the differences between adults and young people. This led on to finding ways of exploring other differences which inevitably existed in any of the meetings because of the rich variety of experiences, beliefs, attitudes and feelings which were present. It was evident to me, when I came to compare the earliest meetings with the later ones, that I had often found myself seeking to avoid issues on which people held different views because they implied the possibility of tension and conflict which might get out of control. I had behaved in ways which drove the problems underground rather than allowing them to be brought to light, articulated, expressed and sometimes learned from.

It was the recognition of the significance of the roles taken in the group which provided the first major insight in this Project. The exploration of what this led to makes up the basis of this report.

The task of these small working groups required that three specific roles be taken in the structure of each group. These were taken (a) by the members of the group; (b) by myself, as Project Officer, and (c) by a visitor.

THE MEMBERS OF THE GROUP

There are pressures on young people to take up their place in the adult world and adults themselves represent important resources to help to do this. It was said earlier that this Project made the initial hypothesis that the focal point of the problems associated with doing this concerns understanding the nature and use of authority. Thus the task of the members of the group was **to study with adults problems arising from the nature and use of authority in society**. It was assumed that this is a task important to young adults and that they came to the group in order to learn something from it. Their individual reasons, of course, differed depending on their own personal circumstances, but the assumption was made that at any one time there were some people present who wanted to carry on with this task.

THE PROJECT OFFICER

This is the most complex role taken in the group and as study of this role took place, it became increasingly apparent that many of the considerations taken in understanding it are relevant to roles taken by adults in work with young people from other settings.

Aspects of the role which emerged as being of significance are as follows:

i.   I was the **initiator of the group** in that I made the original approaches to schools, employers and others who have authority over young adults. The actual membership of the group was not normally determined by me.

ii.   I **defined the task** of the group. In the first place this was done through explaining why the group was called together. I outlined the reasons why those in authority over the members of the group themselves asked for the group to be held, and described my own interest in it, particularly the research considerations which are more fully described later in this section. In the second place, the task was continually defined by those pieces of evidence on which I chose to comment and how I used them in my contributions to the discussion. My own behaviour in relation to the members made a further contribution to the definition of the task.

iii. I was responsible for important aspects of **boundary control** in the group. I arranged the time and place of meetings. I made contact with the representatives of institutions in society who visited the group. I started and finished each session. All these constituted different kinds of boundary control. In addition to this, I bore in mind and used the 'task' and 'sentient' boundaries which are described in the next section of this report. Much of this was done by my being conscious of what transactions were taking place across the different boundaries and using this knowledge in the best way I could to help the group at its work.

iv.   As the person taking the group, I worked to show that I was **concerned with reality** as distinct from fantasy. The kind of questions I asked were designed to help the group examine their fantasies about people in authority and to get to the truth of their previous experience. This meant that I needed to be alert to ways in which the members of groups described such previous experience. To support this aspect of the work of the group a written record was made of what emerged about authority during each session, kept on large sheets of paper; this was kept publicly displayed so that the group could see it in successive sessions. This record was particularly important in final review sessions when groups had opportunities to evaluate the whole experience. There was pressure at this stage either to say that the whole thing had been enormously valuable or alternatively to describe it as being a complete write-off. The public record helped draw attention to what had really been said and what really happened in previous sessions; this was essential if the group was to be helped to come to terms with their experience and what they may have learned.

v.   A significant part of the reality of the group was that I was a representative of authority who was continuously present in the group; for example, in a group drawn from the Probation Service, I represented the probation officers; in a group drawn from work I represented the employers, and in a school or college group I represented the staff. This representation

14

of authority was more complex in situations such as Child Care and will be examined later on. In order to make use of me as a resource in the group situation, the members had to come to terms with me as a representative of that authority under whose auspices the group was meeting.

vi.   In a number of areas I was an **expert** in the group. In these series of groups I had understanding: (a) of the lives and problems of adolescents, especially in Islington; (b) in the study of human behaviour, within and between groups, and (c) of the nature of authority and problems arising from how it is used in society. My resources as an expert were offered to the group for them to use in whatever way they might choose.

vii.   I also provided a **model of behaviour** for the group in that the kind of leadership I gave in studying problems of authority was public and open to examination by the group. The way I listened to what people said, the way I struggled with the difficulties the group encountered and shared these with the members rather than keeping problems to myself or throwing them back for the group to work at alone, were all open to be copied or commented upon by the group. Probably the most common difficulties with which the groups had to cope arose from failures which occurred during the life of the group; failures arising from my actions, the members themselves and the visitors. It was important in the first place that I behave in such a way as to accept responsibility for my own failures: I could not pretend that the difficulties which were consequent to that failure were mine alone, but I had to recognise that the group was affected as a whole and we needed to grapple with those difficulties together. Where other people's failures had to be coped with, I again behaved in such a way as to demonstrate that the consequences of the failure were a problem for the group as a whole and as such must be worked at by us all.

In essence, this model is one which invited members of the group to participate with me rather than to be passive recipients. By providing a model of this kind the way the task of the group could be performed was demonstrated. Since the performance of this particular task called for a different kind of relationship between me, the members of the groups and the visitors, from that which may have been encountered in most of their previous experience, the ability of the group to adapt the model to their own use affected how much the members of the group gained from the sessions.

viii. I am **adult** myself and so represented other adults. This meant that I had some positions and responsibilities to which members of the group might not yet have attained; I had experience of such problems as leaving school, taking up work, getting married, being a father, a voter, and so on. These aspects of my experience were available to the group to be used by its members in whatever way they wished, including maybe to ignore them.

ix.   I was a person who was engaged in **research** into the lives of young adults. This meant that I was concerned to try and use sociological, psychological and theological concepts to understand what happened in these groups in a way which was not necessarily always relevant to my immediate task in the group. Since that task was to help the members to learn, there were occasions when I had to neglect lines of thought which might be important to research side of the Project, in favour of the job in hand. My problem here was to judge what would be helpful to the group and what could be important to me alone. The fact that I exposed myself to the possibility of making mistakes each time I made such judgements could be important for the group's learning about the use of authority. My capacity to acknowledge such mistakes from which I tried to recover, provided a part of the model described in part vii.

x.   Finally, and rather differently, part of what I brought to the group was myself as a **person**. This is the result of the combination of my own experiences from birth with my inherited characteristics which cause me to respond to situations in a particular way. The responses which are features of my person needed to be distinguished from those responses which were part of the role in order that the group might be helped to learn about authority from the way in which I used it myself. I am also a Christian with my experience of a relationship with God through Christ and some experience of love, forgiveness and grace which arise from this particular relationship and my relationship with other Christians in the Church and outside it.

THE VISITORS

i.   In the first place, each visitor was the **representative of an institution** in society, invited to come to the group to speak on behalf of other people belonging to that institution. He was therefore identified in the eyes of the group with the actions and behaviour of other members of that institution who may have been encountered in the past experience of individual young people in the group or their friends, and was expected to accept responsibility for explaining such things to the group. Where the members of the group had little previous experience of his institution, he had to find ways of conveying to them its task and describing the problems encountered in carrying it out.

The visitor demonstrated his or her link with his institution or professional grouping by being conscious of his authority as its representative in the group, and by behaving in such a way as to help the members
of the group to become aware of his identification with his colleagues.
As they learned to perceive the authority of a visitor and how he used it
in the group, so the task of the group was carried out. This meant that
the visitor, if he were to stay in role, had to be able to cope with whatever feelings the members of the group had towards his institution and
try to help work them through.

If, by his behaviour, the visitor failed to communicate that he was
the representative of the institution whence he was invited, he was seen
in some other light. The most obvious one was as a representative of
adults in general. This implied, in the context of the group, that the
differences between the structures of society and the tasks they are set
up to perform are less important than differences between generations.
One of the consequences of this impression was to cause young adults,
particularly those still at school, to feel frustrated in their desire to
take their own place in the adult world.

11. Besides being a representative of a structure, each visitor is a person
who has been taking a role within an organisational structure. As a
person, he has a combination of experiences arising throughout his life
which affect the way in which he responds to the situations he encounters.
As in the case of the Project Officer, when he also meets the group, an
element of what is available for exploration is the difference between
those parts of his behaviour which express his role and those parts which
are expressions of his own person. The importance of this has been
noted in the earlier discussion of the Project Officer's role and will be
returned to again in the exploration of adulthood.

THEORETICAL EXAMINATION OF THE GROUPS

From the beginning of the Project it has proved necessary to be able to use
conceptual tools which enabled my developing experience to be explored and
understood. In the first place, each series of group meetings was not held
in a vacuum but everyone, including myself, came to them from different
situations and when we left a series, we went back to those situations. This
can be illustrated diagrammatically as in Figure 1. This kind of diagram
enables us to look at a series of meetings as a unit, aiming to effect some
change, as a result of what happened in it, in those who joined a series and
who left it when it was over. The process which caused the change can be
called the conversion process. More precision can be achieved by distin-
guishing more accurately who joins and who leaves. By knowing what change
has taken place in those who leave the group it is possible to form some

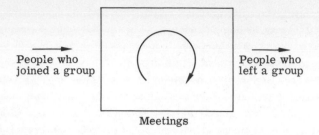

Meetings

Figure 1. A series of meetings

conclusions about the series and its success or failure. The intakes to a series were: young people, myself and a number of visitors. Together we examined and explored problems associated with the nature and use of authority. At the end of a series some people left having learned something about authority; others left having learned nothing. Some of the latter probably fell out before the scheduled end was reached.

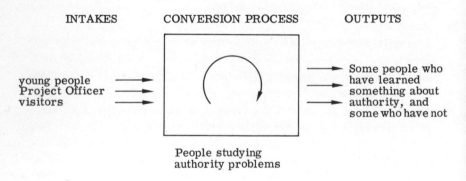

People studying authority problems

Figure 2. The diagram more precisely applied to this project

It is important to note that it is not assumed that everybody always left a session having learned about authority — in fact it probably never happened like that. But if the groups were to carry out the task for which they were created then some learning had to take place on someone's part. At the worst there were occasions when no-one learned or when I was the only person who learned; there may have been others in which I did not learn but someone else did and since each individual series of groups was primarily designed to help the members rather than myself, that was a better situation than the first two.

This way of looking at the life of groups is part of a general theory of organisations which has been evolved over the last thirty years or so, called the 'open system' theory. This theory postulates that an open system exists

18

by exchanging materials with its environment. It imports materials, processes them in its conversion process and exports the final product plus the waste materials. This import-conversion-export process is the work the enterprise must carry out if it is to live.

The particular approach to open-systems thinking which I have been using is that derived from the work of Dr A K Rice and his colleagues at the Tavistock Institute. [8] This approach highlights the importance of the work of a group and the problems which arise from this, especially arising from the fact that any group which continues in existence is not only carrying out its work but also to some extent meeting the needs of its members as persons. In examining this problem Dr Rice evolved the concept of **Primary Task.** Rice came to define primary task as **that task which an enterprise must perform if it is to survive.** The 'primary' label is a statement of the relationship of the work to the organisation of the enterprise, and is not a judgemental comment on the subjective or moral value of particular aspects of the work.

This conception of primary task means that any group or enterprise which continues in existence, by definition has a primary task, whether it is articulated or not, whether people are aware of it or not.

Dr Rice points out that a very important function of the leadership of an institution is to define the institution's primary task. In particular he demonstrates that leadership defines the task not simply in words and statements, but more importantly through behaviour, decisions and actions which affect the life and activities within a group or enterprise.

In the groups in this Project I was the designated leader: because I was also responsible for the whole project, I personally had two tasks in every group — of helping the young people and of doing research. At times these tasks clashed and I needed a way of sorting out the priorities in such situations. In such instances, the declared primary task of the group, rather than of the Project as a whole, took precedence because it was on the basis of that task that young people joined the group in the first place. If the groups had not been helping with the overall research task, I would have had to stop them and seek another way of working. As has already been said, the primary task of the groups was spelled out before they started, as being: to provide opportunities for a group's members to meet adults and explore with them problems arising from the nature and use of authority. It was through my behaviour and the decisions that I took in a group that the task was reiterated session by session. As the members of the group observed my behaviour they came to understand the task for themselves. As they did this, they in their turn were able to adopt the behaviour and actions which constituted leadership functions in enabling the task to be carried out. Nevertheless, as designated leader I remained responsible for what happened in a group.   I was responsible for deciding whether or not the declared task was being performed in the series. On the one occasion when I did not believe it was being carried out I ended the series before its scheduled conclusion.

Returning to the open system model illustrated earlier, it is quickly apparent that the most significant actions, which can therefore be seen as the leadership actions, are those which affect what comes into the group and therefore what goes out. In Rice's terms such actions control the boundaries of a group or enterprise. These functions define the limits of what can happen within a group and how it relates to its environment; they also define what aspects of the total environment are significant to the existence of the group. It is important to stress that in these terms leadership is not solely vested in an individual but can be exercised by anyone who acts in a way which controls a boundary in relation to a group's task.

This can be represented diagrammatically by drawing a double boundary around a group, as in Figure 3.

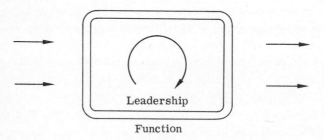

Figure 3. The leadership function of an open system model

This illustrates an area between the internal world of a group and its external environment at which there is a pause for reflection, a region of regulation, at which decisions are taken. To exercise leadership is thus to look outwards to the environment and inwards to the internal world of a group and to act in a way which attempts to relate the two to each other. In the example given of the first session with the printers, my remarks about the company made in response to the remarks about liberal studies at college, constituted a leadership function because they indicated that the significant part of the environment for the life of this group was the company. Therefore the important intakes were young people in their role of employees, not young people in their role of college students.

Thus their experience of college needed to be examined and understood in relation to their employment in this instance, though it might be approached and studied from other points of view elsewhere. Such an observation could have been made by anyone in the group who perceived its relevance. In fact the final sessions were specifically designed to help all the members of a group to do just this for themselves and thus learn about authority from their experience of it.

What has not been explored up to now, yet has been shown by the examples given to be very important, are the relationships in which all those who came to a group were engaged.   It is necessary now to draw the kind of diagram which illustrates this by representing the individual members, as in Figure 4.

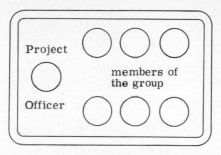

Figure 4. A small working group in the Project, during the first or last stages of a series, ie without a visitor

We must now bear in mind the fact that what is illustrated is not a static situation but is in fact a dynamic one to which the relationships contribute in their turn.   To start with I had other relationships in that I belonged to another relevant group at the same time as belonging to the one illustrated — through my membership of the Grubb Institute; without which the small working group would never have come into existence in the first place. This can be illustrated in Figure 5.   This is a description which has some approximation to reality because it was clear that I was always regarded as different from the rest of the members of the group.   But it was evident that this somewhat more elaborate description fell far short of being a useful way to interpret the whole situation.

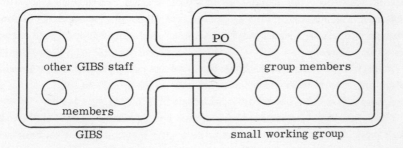

Figure 5. The group seen as an intergroup meeting between a staff member of GIBS and the group's own members

TASK AND SENTIENT GROUPS

In Example III, the visit of the probation officer, it was evident that the groups being **experienced** by those present were of a different kind from the Grubb Institute and the probation service. In Example IV, of the headmaster's visit, all boundaries of any kind were obliterated. We therefore need concepts which enable us to think about different kinds of groups.

A human being is seldom if ever the member of only one group. At any one moment we are the members of a whole range of groups: our families, the institution for which we work, departments or sections within that institution, professional associations or trades unions, social or sports clubs are a few examples. Rice, with his colleague Dr E J Miller, [9] offers two further concepts which enable the complexity of the situation to be explored and which can be used in the context of this project. These are the notions of **task** and **sentient** groups.

A **task group** is a group comprised of the individuals directly engaged in the performance of a particular job of work. Together they supply and use the human and physical resources necessary to carry out that task. The members of a typing pool plus their supervisor constitute a task group, similarly the fitters and mechanics in a garage plus the foreman or other supervisor together make up a task group. Where the task involves human clients or customers they may also be a part of a task group: for example, a doctor and his patient or a teacher and his class.

Task groups have a number of significant features. First the group is formed round **a task**. This may or may not be precisely defined but the group's effectiveness is judged by its success in carrying out that task. Secondly, the way a task group organises itself is determined by the **activities** which must be performed to carry out the task. These activities are grouped together in roles which can be taken by different individuals. No individual is indispensable in a task group, providing his role is taken by someone with the specific skills necessary to carry out that part of the task contributed by that role. Thirdly, **the boundaries** of the task group are defined in relation to the nature of the task. Times, places, membership, equipment, relevant behaviour and so on, are all determined by considering how best to further the task of the group.

In principle, once a task group has finished its work it can disband since it has no further reason to stay in existence.

A **sentient group** is a group to which an individual gives loyalty, in which he invests feelings (**sentiment**) and to which he has a sense of belonging. It is a group which a person talks of as 'we'. Any group to which we feel we belong has sentience for us. The sentience may be strong, as it is with our families, it may be short lived as in the case of a group of people met together at a conference or on holiday. It may be a continued but limited sentience, such as the group of people with whom we work.

The development of sentience in a group can be attributed to the development inside each member of an image of the group which is invested with positive feelings. In this way an aggregate of individuals becomes for each member a social entity which is valued and protected, to a greater or lesser degree. It can be felt to continue to exist when the members of the group are physically separated from each other, since the image of the group inside each member can persist and may affect his behaviour in other situations.

Sometimes the circumstances in which an individual finds himself make him aware of being a member of more than one sentient group. For example, promotion at work can increase a man's status at home, which is pleasant; it may involve a conflict of loyalties which entails the denial of one affiliation in an attempt to extricate oneself from a painful situation, as may sometimes happen to a Christian youth leader in a secular youth club. Professional associations, trades unions and employers associations, political parties and churches are all examples of important and often powerful kinds of sentient groups, some of them operating with sanctions and controls which have the force of law.

The raison d'etre of a sentient group is the well-being of its members; the ways it organises itself and its activities, and defines its boundaries all have this end in view. It exists to meet the emotional needs of its members for a sense of belonging, acceptance, security, fellowship and a sense of purpose. A sentient group may have no other task than the fostering of its own ethos and ideals. But this is not necessarily so; it may also be a task group with a defined task, in which case the objectives of the task group are themselves the focus of sentience. In this way carrying out the task meets some of the emotional needs of the group's members. In fact any task group which is going to be successful needs to mobilise the degree of sentience which will enable its members to support and cooperate with each other in the fulfilment of the task.

It is one of the functions of task leadership to mobilise the required sentience for task performance, and also to control the relationships which develop between task and sentient groups in such a way as to facilitate that task performance.

Using the notation which indicates the boundaries of **task groups** thus:

and sentient group boundaries, which differ from and are in addition to the task boundaries, thus

it becomes possible to elaborate the diagram as in Figure 6, where the sentient groups are those of adults and young people. The group can now

23

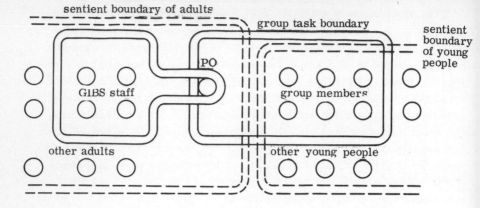

Figure 6. A group seen as an intergroup meeting of adults and young people

be seen as a representative meeting between adults and young people, as well as a meeting between a Grubb Institute staff member and the group.

When a visitor came to a group, he or she was also an adult and fitted into the boundary alongside me as another representative of the adult world, elaborating the diagram to show his membership of another institution such as the Metropolitan Police or the staff of a school.

In these last three diagrams we have been taking for granted that we are illustrating one specific point in a process. What has also been taken for granted is that each group met as part of the overall work of an institution: say a school, a firm or the probation and after-care service, which provided the environment of a group. It has been indicated in the example of the young printers that this context was important. This needs now to be brought into the diagram to make it more complete. This is done in Figure 7.

What is shown to be of key importance by looking at the diagram, are the points at which boundaries cross each other, since these represent points at which decisions were taken and authority was exercised by those in leadership positions. If members of a group were to learn about authority, how these decisions were made, the grounds for making them, and their consequences, were of great significance to them because these were the raw material for study. A brief glance at both Figures 7 and 8 which introduces a visitor to the group, shows that the task boundaries cross each other at a number of different points while the sentient boundaries do not.

The visitor came in with me and therefore derived some of his authority in the group from this fact. For this reason he is enclosed within the Project Officer/GIBS boundary. Since I had met visitors before they came to the group, some relationship was already established when we entered the

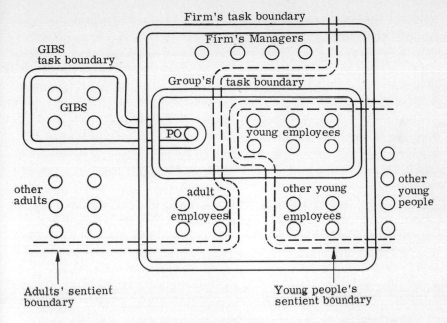

Figure 7. A group of young employees taken for a firm, showing Project Officer's links with GIBS and other adults; also group members' links with other young people

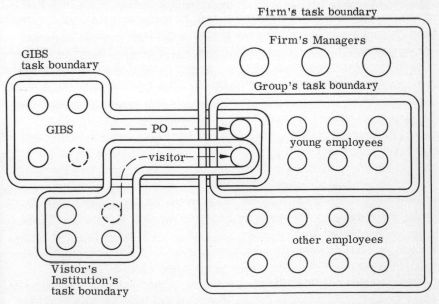

Figure 8. A group of young employees with a visitor. The sentient boundaries have not been included in order to keep the diagram clear, although in some circumstances they apply and cut across the task boundaries

25

group and this links us in the diagram. The visitor was also in the group in a different role from myself since he represented the group of people with whom he worked. It was important to the group's learning about authority that these different roles were able to be perceived by the young people. Thus the group was a complex system of relationships which linked the members of the group with other young people and with the adult world.

It is important to note that in the structure of a firm the young people were able to refer to the models of adult behaviour of other employees to help them to decide how to behave in this situation. This is of course not the case in the institutions such as schools where the only colleagues to whom reference can be made are other young people.

In terms of looking outwards from the group into adult society, after a full series of meetings a group had met several different visitors and had opportunities to look at that number of institutions in society and learn about them in a way which enabled them to examine their own position as young adults in relation to these institutions. As they put all this experience together, they had a simple model which could begin to help them understand the nature of the society in which they were taking their place.

But crucial to this taking place was the necessity for anyone who discerned it to point to the evidence which helped those involved to try to identify their role in the group. This particularly involved the adults understanding their own role and task in society and sticking to expressing this in their behaviour in the group whatever the pressure to do something else. The problems arising from this are explored at length later.

In the examples given of sessions with visitors some important illustrations of the diagrams emerge. In the example of the probation officer the task boundaries became obscured and the sentient boundaries were clearly apparent; the notation of the diagram could have been reversed with the task boundaries becoming interrupted while the sentient boundaries became dominant. The policeman began in a way which seemed to indicate that the sentient boundaries might be important but because the feelings which came out were close to feelings for the police, the task boundaries became the established ones. The headmaster made the sentient boundary around the group and himself the significant one because he so dominated the situation that the students felt themselves to be young, inexperienced and inadequate in his presence and handed over all control to him. The nurse on the other hand was able to maintain an awareness of the situation so that the fact that she was both a nurse and an adult woman was not lost sight of.

It was evident that the sessions which were most creative were those in which the different boundaries were able to be taken into account by all concerned. In the terms of this Project, to be 'in role' meant that a person behaved in a way that enabled the task boundaries which concerned him to be taken especially into account by others as well as by himself. This behaviour was probably not always consciously directed in such a way. What I found was that where I was able to understand what was happening in a group, I was able to use my recognition of these boundaries in ways which had a releasing effect on the resources of those present. This may have been by direct reference to the boundaries or it may have been by my formulating a question or comment in the light of what I had seen.

The significant point about the role of an adult in these sessions was to recognise that the task of the group required not simply the enumeration or exercise of the skills of one's professional group — a fireman did not come to fight fires — but the exploration of what it meant to be an adult who had to use such skills as he had. This involved describing one's own feelings in working situations and talking about how one used, controlled or ignored such feelings. In other words 'to stay in role' in the group involved mobilising both one's resources as an adult and the skills and experience derived from one's working life, and using these together in the performance of the group's task. It was evident that many people, including myself, found this a difficult thing to do consistently.

The problems which adults encountered in staying in role, the results of their success and failure to do that in terms of the way it affected the young people in the groups, and my own understanding of these issues constitute the major exploration of this report. Underlying it all was the continual application of the model illustrated in Figures 7 and 8. These diagrams are therefore of considerable importance to understanding the following chapters.

NOTES

(1)	Mary Morse	Unattached	Pelican 1965
(2)	G Goetschius and J Tash	Working with Unattached Youth	Routledge and Kegan Paul 1967
(3)	E M and M Eppel	Adolescents and Morality	Routledge and Kegan Paul 1966
(4)	M Schofield	The Sexual Behaviour of Young People	Longmans Green 1965
(5)	D Downes	Delinquent Solution	Routledge and Kegan Paul 1966
(6)	P Willmott	Adolescent Boys in East London	Routledge and Kegan Paul 1966
(7)	G Burton	People Matter More Than Things	Hodder 1965
(8)	A K Rice	The Enterprise and its Environment	Tavistock Publications 1963
	A K Rice	Learning for Leadership	Tavistock Publications 1965
(9)	E J Miller and A K Rice	Systems of Organization	Tavistock Publications 1967

27

3. The Behaviour of Young People in the Groups

As was said earlier, fourteen different groups of young people have taken part in the Project, 143 persons in all. The groups' members were aged from 14 up to 21 with the majority being between 15 and 17. They varied from those who were socially and academically disadvantaged, some of them being delinquent, to young people of high academic ability and of stable employment and social background. It is from this very diversity that a view of the situation of young people in general has emerged including some understanding of their beliefs and attitudes about the adult world, and their expectations of what adults might be able to do to help them.

ATTENDANCE

In getting together any group in whatever setting, I always made it clear to those who contemplated joining that attendance was not compulsory, nor could I compel even those who opted to join the group to continue to come. In some cases such as schools, the institution from which members were drawn did have sanctions which could have been used should those in leadership positions wish to do so, but the groups were always set up in a way which gave the members options which did not necessarily involve risking those sanctions being applied. For example, those who attended a group run by the probation and after-care service had the continuing option of reporting to their officer or attending the group; in this way, absenting themselves from the group did not of itself run the risk of becoming a breach of the probation order. All but one of the school and college groups were timetabled as an option to another subject or activity and in some cases after a session or two in the group the occasional pupil did opt for the alternative. The most problematical groups were the two in which the range of options was widest in a paradoxical way, in that the bodies sponsoring the group, a youth club and the Children's Department, provided no alternatives within their own structure and the groups met in the members' leisure time. This meant that members of the group had to match attendance against the whole range of alternatives available week by week, be it what films were on at the local cinema, visiting sick relatives, or being caught up in 'chats' with one's friends or family. The best way of describing this situation is to say that these two groups were not seen as taking place within an authority structure.

The choice about attending had therefore to be reiterated every time the group was due to meet. Not surprisingly, these two groups both failed to last the planned course because insufficient support was provided. What was interesting was that in both cases meetings were able to take place for nearly three months altogether, though with falling numbers; the Children's Department group had been planned to meet for six months altogether, the youth club group was planned for three. No-one came to the final meeting, all other planned meetings having taken place, though with a steadily dwindling attendance.

The point to be drawn from this is that where young people recognised and felt themselves to be a part of the structure within which the group met, whatever their individual feelings about that structure, they were able to sustain attendance for periods of up to six months even where alternatives arising outside the structure were very attractive to them (eg Arsenal playing at home). There were fluctuations in attendance during the course of the meetings and there were some significant factors which seemed to influence this. The most influential of these was my own attendance. All but one of the groups which had to miss a session because of my own absence (whatever the reason for that absence) were marked by very variable attendance subsequently; in the case of the Children's Department group my own absence for two weeks when on holiday was clearly the final straw in a fluid and uncertain situation. In three other cases stability was regained after three or four weeks. In one case my absence had no effect on attendance at all. The members of this group were drawn from employment.

Besides my own behaviour, it was evident that the behaviour of the visiting adults also affected the attendance of the members of the groups. Where a visitor raised feelings of anger and frustration which were not able to be worked at, the attendance at the following sessions was likely to fall. It was not simply the raising of such feelings which had this effect, but the failure of the visitor to work at them with the group. For example, a trades unionist visited a group of young employees and only succeeded in conveying a picture of defensiveness against the problems of young people such as themselves: he implied that though the unions were prepared to let young people join, the difficulties they encountered as employees were insoluble by union leaders. In frustration one young man finally threw up his hands and said 'All we want is a job which we know is fair'. He attended no further meetings after that. Following the visit to the youth club group of a child care officer who carried out a case-work interview with one of those present rather than explaining

29

why child care officers adopted certain policies, half those present did not come again. They did not feel able to face the risk of being dealt with as their mate had been handled, so took the easiest and seemingly safest course out. The relationship between the behaviour of visiting adults and the behaviour of the members of groups has constituted a major area of study and is described in subsequent chapters.

ENDING

A pattern of behaviour which was frequently evident in these working groups was a great difficulty in coping with ending the series. In the earliest groups I only planned one session for review purposes. Attendances at this session invariably dropped sharply, the seeming desire being to cut the series short rather than go through the pain and stress of working right up to the end. An alternative way of dealing with this was to ask that the series be continued indefinitely and attempt to avoid ending by pretending that it was not necessary to end. In subsequent groups I allocated first two sessions, and finally three, to review. This meant that the problem of ending could begin to be faced with some time to work at it; in some cases this was from almost three quarters of the way through the series. The effect of giving more time to this was to decrease both the attempt to cut things short and the attempt to prolong the series of meetings. This is not to say that the ending was easy: I found that I had to carry a considerable strain at the actual point of ending the last session, but the model set in closing the session at the stated time, packing up and leaving was important in terms of helping the young adults themselves cope with their part of the ending. I was frequently conscious of how easy it would have been to hang around chatting letting everyone else drift away leaving me as the last to go, but I was also aware of how this would have been to shift the burden of making the final break onto others. I came to the conclusion that I could best help a group learn about ending by taking full responsibility for my own part in it. If they wished to hang around with each other they were quite free to do that. For this reason I always left the last session promptly and with as little fuss as possible.

THE DIFFERENT SETTINGS

Each of the different settings from which groups were drawn seemed to have its own influence on the behaviour of the group members. What was evident to me were the assumptions about relating to adults which the young people made as they came to the group. Most marked was the pattern evident in those from schools. In the preliminary sessions I was always treated to detailed accounts of the awfulness of their teachers who were portrayed as being unpredictable, malicious, violent and sometimes unscrupulous. Girls told stories of how male teachers had made oblique references to aspects of sexual behaviour, and boys talked of violence perpetrated by some staff members. I experienced this sort of discussion as a massive invitation to collude with the groups against their schools, and would tell them so. We would then attempt to understand why they needed to do this. When challenged as to whether all their teachers were like this, the groups usually agreed that only some were — but mostly continued to talk about only this section of the school staff.

Subsequent to a session of this sort, school groups fell into silence and apathy. Visitors would find that groups had difficulty in knowing how to ask questions or follow them up. There was a continual invitation to the adults present to take over and run the session, with one or two young people being put forward to make sure the flow was kept up while the remainder sheltered behind them. The only group which presented serious problems of members leaving the room during sessions was a school group and they did this on three different occasions, including the one described earlier. Absenteeism from school groups also tended to be rather higher than from others, as was late arrival at the beginning of sessions.

The school groups contained both early leavers and some who intended to stay on for a fifth year, though members were mostly early leavers. None of the groups were wholly made up of those staying on for a fifth year; three groups were entirely composed of early leavers. There were no very marked differences between these groups apart from a tendency to greater apathy in the groups made up entirely of leavers.

The assumptions which all those groups appeared to make was that adults were expected to take over and control the situation and to relieve the young people of responsibility for what went on. Adults were seen as having all the authority, young people were felt to have none. My feeling was that the attempts to capture me with their vivid tales in preliminary sessions were intended to try to get me to align myself with them against those who might be hostile to them in the belief that my authority, as it was believed to be, might be used as a form of protection. My own behaviour presented considerable problems to those who made such assumptions because I refused to believe in their own lack of capacities and skill, and also refused to deny my own. In some cases groups were unable to come wholly to terms with me throughout a whole term of meetings. The making of these assumptions also presented difficulties for many of the adults who visited the groups; they easily fell into long discourses, responding to the slightest prompting in order to avoid any periods of silence. Though they personally may have felt that the session passed off without disaster (though only few thought such meetings went well), remarks made by the young people indicated that they had a poor opinion of what took place. One group remarked, 'It was just like Jackanory on the BBC. All right for five-year-olds'. As they spoke they attempted

31

to deny that they had had any influence in causing the session to develop as it did.

The problem seemed to be that young people at school were unable to cope with uncertainty and the stress which this entailed. They experienced such feelings as destructive and to be fled from, believing that I, who attempted to confront uncertainty and to tolerate stress with them, was being punitive The effect of believing this was to make it extremely hard to use constructively the disagreements and differences which were obvious in such situations because the young people were making the assumption that such conflicts would inevitably destroy them; having made such an assumption, it was then almost impossible for them to put it to the test because of the risks which were believed to be entailed. Absenteeism, lateness, silence and flight from the room were all devices for coping with the problems stemming from those beliefs.

The groups closest in behaviour to the school groups were the two taken from further education, both made up of junior civil servants and employees of public corporations. They were mainly aged between 17 and 19. It was again apparent that both these groups were broadly making the assumption that in the group situation the adults had all the authority and they as young people had none. Though both groups were more articulate than the school groups and they were better at prompting the right questions or putting in comments, they still expected the visitors and myself to carry the load, and were exceedingly hard pressed when we either refused or failed to do this. In both groups the final sessions were marked by long periods of silence as the members and I tried to review what had happened and what relevance it had to their lives in other situations, because I tried to avoid collusion with the belief that I was the only person who had anything of value to contribute.

There was some difference between each of the two college groups in their capacity to cope with the problem. One group had mainly left school following GCE 'O' level and had been at work for about two years, the other had all stayed on to the sixth form and had been at work for just over six months. The first group showed a greater awareness of having skills of their own and, though a number of them coped with it by going absent, the majority showed some capacity to struggle with the problem of using them. The second group found themselves stuck in regular, almost silent, attendance feeling unable either to fight or to flee.

The most contrasted behaviour was displayed by those groups which were drawn from employment, the groups of van boys, warehousemen and printers. The assumption which was made by groups meeting in this setting was that they had something to contribute to the meetings and they usually made the effort required to make such contributions. They seemed to be able to cope with much greater degrees of uncertainty than young people of a similar age in a different setting. Problems about depression and despair were better able to be articulated, and aggression was able to be used more creatively in working both with me and with visitors. Absenteeism was very low and lateness almost non-existent except in instances clearly beyond the individual's control such as a van-boy's lorry not returning from a lengthy delivery round. These young employees seemed to have a greater awareness of having authority themselves in relation to adults and were also more sensitive to the real authority that adults had; that is to say, they did not attribute omnipotence to adults so easily. On the basis of this, the kind of relationships established in the sessions tended to be more realistic about the available resources for work than those made in educational institutions. This resulted in a greater sense of freedom for all concerned including myself and the visiting adults.

It seemed that young people meeting at their place of work were able to behave in these ways because they had a sense of security which was different from that of the other groups. This made it easier to make more realistic criticisms about the institution and its leaders, without the caricatures usually offered by school-based groups. They also found it easier to understand my relationship to the work of the group and therefore with them.

At first I felt that these differences might stem from the fact that members of employment-based groups were older than school groups and could therefore be reasonably expected to be more mature in their behaviour. As experience developed it became apparent that this was not the whole answer. The oldest groups I took were the ones in further education, but their behaviour in that setting was less mature than others who were younger in years, but who met in conjunction with their employment. In one instance a boy who had behaved very destructively in one of the school groups turned up at a firm where I was also working with a group of young employees. His behaviour was still exuberant, but now he was able to handle his outbursts more constructively and because of his exuberance was able to be a valuable member of the group. The space between his leaving school and appearing in the group at work was just over two weeks. It seemed that being at work gave him a new basis for his behaviour.

A confirmation of the way assumptions related to structures within which groups met arose in the group of young printers quoted earlier (Example I). During that session I was aware of the mounting apathy and pressure on me. I was trying to find ways of helping the group understand what the meetings were about and felt that I was failing to communicate anything. Then the boy made his remark about lessons at college. This gave me the clue to why I was feeling the way I was. I was being seen as a teacher and a college structure was being constructed around me. I made my remark about being on the firm's premises and meeting in the firm's time. This led to discussion of problems encountered at work, relations with overseers, union leaders and colleagues; the following forty-five minutes were lively and hard working. It was hard to believe that this was the same group of people who had opened the session in such a dull fashion. It seemed that by drawing attention to the relation of the group to their firm I had enabled them to discover a task and rôle in the group which gave them a sense of identity as members of a structure in which they had some confidence and for which they felt considerable enthusiasm.

There was a similarity between the youth club group and the Children's Department group, both of which met in the members' spare time. The attendance and ultimate failure of both has already been mentioned, but there is a further point which seems to me to be significant. This was the level of anxiety which was present in both groups, stemming from the great uncertainty about who would attend each session. The boundaries and the structure were in each case either indiscernible or at most insufficiently clear. The members of the group could not identify a task from which to draw a real sense of identity. This caused the behaviour of those who attended to be uncertain. They tried to cope with this by expecting the adults present to alleviate the problem. Partly this was a realistic expectation, because I had seriously underestimated the problem of working in people's spare time, and had not taken sufficient measures to help them, but partly it was carried to an unrealistic point by the extent of the invitation given to the adults to take over and 'run' the meetings. This combination certainly contributed to the ultimate folding up of both groups.

YOUNG MEN AND YOUNG WOMEN

Half of the fourteen groups have contained members of both sexes, all the rest were entirely male groups. No groups were made up entirely of girls. It is difficult to arrive at any generalisations on the basis of the evidence available from these groups, though there was a very slight tendency for girls in mixed school groups to be more silent and withdrawn than their male colleagues. It was also evident in mixed school groups that either the girls would lead the discussion or the boys would; seldom was everyone free to participate without anyone being suppressed by the members of the opposite sex.

There were also differences observable on the basis of sex in the two further education groups. Here the girls were used by the group to give the initial leadership in asking the early questions of visitors, the boys always remaining silent till some time after the session started. There seemed to be some expectation that if the visiting adult proved difficult to deal with, an attractive and seemingly confident girl would be less likely to be roughly handled than a young man. The point here was the fact that what was **expected**

34

was hostility from adults and the use of girls was a way of coping with that apprehension.

In terms of general attitudes towards authority and representatives of the adult world, girls were slightly more compliant and where such compliance had apparently failed, tended towards despair and depression; boys on the other hand tended to be angry and aggressive. These remarks might be interpreted as indications of some support for education of boys and girls separately; this would be mistaken, for I believe what is shown is that the behaviour described indicates insufficient working through of the matters at issue and therefore calls for more concentration on it rather than less.

THE SELECTION OF VISITORS

The kind of visitors each group selected show important factors in how young people feel about authority. The groups were all introduced to young people in ways which indicated that they were intended to help find out something about the problems of using authority in adult society. There were variations in the exact wording used depending on the different circumstances, but the basic message was the same. At the end of the first session or early in the second the members of the group compiled the list of people they wished to meet. In most cases they drew up a list which was longer than could be used, which they then reduced through discussion amongst themselves. The result was that representatives of twenty-nine different kinds of adult occupations were invited to visit groups. A number of occupations were asked to a number of different groups and this is indicated in the following table, arranged in order of frequency:

Policemen (13)	Football Manager (1)
Prison Officers (10)	Traffic Warden (1)
Magistrates (8)	Police Surgeon (1)
Borough Councillors (6)	House Mother (1)
Employers (6)	Educational Psychologist (1)
Teachers (5)	Cinema Manager (1)
Probation Officers (4)	Security Officer (1)
Priests (4)	Schools Special Officer (1)
Nurses (3)	Member of Parliament (1)
Careers Advisory Officers (3)	Publican (1)
Parents (3)	Trades Unionist (1)
Football Referees (2)	Doctor (1)
Child Care Officers (2)	Soldier (1)
Firemen (2)	Ex-Prisoner (1)
Leader of coloured community (2)	

Total 87 visits (in some cases a visitor came to 2 groups)

In order to get a specific visitor, once a list had been compiled I would approach the head of the appropriate institution and ask him to send a representative; for example to get a policeman I would approach the Commander of the local Metropolitan Police Division; for a prison officer I went to the governor of the nearest prison. For such people as priests or the MP I went in the first instance to the head of the local parish or the constituency member. It is no surprise that policemen, prison officers and magistrates head the list. In the first place all the groups have begun from the point of seeing authority primarily concerned with punishment and control. What has been interesting has been how groups have moved away from that simplistic view of the nature of authority and have brought it nearer and nearer to their own everyday experience. This has meant that authority figures were less and less prejudged as 'bad objects'. Borough Councillors have figured surprisingly frequently, indicating greater local government awareness than might have been expected. It is also somewhat surprising to find that priests were invited as frequently as probation officers. It may also be unexpected to find parents figuring in the list at all, given the fantasies which adults have of the feelings of young people about their parents. [2]

What was important, which emerged in the two groups which planned visitors for a six-month period, was that given time to work through the more punitive authority figures (few of whom were encountered in most people's day-to-day lives), the groups would move towards inviting in the authority figures most closely involved with them in reality. The Children's Department group planned to meet a child care officer, a house mother from a residential unit and the mother and father of adolescent children. The group of van-boys and young employees met a trades unionist and an employer; in the last two sessions of the series they asked one of the directors and the managing director of their own firm to come in to talk over their positions in the company with them.

Given the chance of developing in this way, the relationship between adults and young people could increasingly be defined in roles within task systems recognised and accepted by both parties, which then allowed the beliefs and attitudes of each sentient group to be mobilised as resources within those task systems so that work and development could take place. It was in this kind of situation that the support and resources which I was able to give were most directly apparent to the young people (and also, incidentally, to the visiting adults). In this sort of setting I was more obviously concerned with their real problems and less obviously a researcher doing a study likely only to be of interest to myself and others.

CHANGES OVER THE THREE YEARS

Since the Project began in 1966 there has been a noticeable shift in the behaviour of young people. In the autumn of that year there was evidence that most young people, particularly those from a working class background, tended to have a capacity to fight problems and difficulties. In a few cases this aggressive capacity was grossly misdirected in terms of the problems of growing up as responsible members of society and was evident in vandalism and delinquency. Nevertheless, where this capacity could be put to constructive use, dramatic development frequently took place. In the last year this capacity to fight has largely disappeared. What has taken its place is a lethargy and bewilderment which soon dissolves into depression and a state of stasis or inertia. The anger which could be creatively used two or three years ago has been turned inwards on themselves and they have become imprisoned in apathy. In the early sessions groups usually asked to meet a policeman, a prison officer, a probation officer and a magistrate. From 1968 onwards they seldom asked to meet so many concerned with the maintenance of law and order and began to include people more representative of the caring professions and education. Interestingly enough this change has coincided with the rise of student militancy. It seems that the battle is now being carried on in another quarter leaving different feelings to be coped with by working class young men. But the problem which has remained has been still that of coping with the hostility of adults.

The change has meant that the demands on visiting adults have changed and their job of helping the groups has in fact become more difficult since the members are not coming forward to take up issues with them, but are already fleeing from them. Problems presented have been about despair, depression and feeling trapped: the ways used to present the issues have seldom been direct but by such allusion as feeling lost or falling into morose silence. The pressure on adults to behave more seductively to win young people back to them has been enormous, particularly given the propensity for the members of the caring and teaching professions to try to 'fill up' silence with 'friendly' talk. This resulted in the adults failing to mobilise the appropriate resources to tackle the real problems experienced by the young people. I found that despite increased experience, it became harder to work in these groups rather than easier.

ATTITUDES TO ADULTS

In calling a group together, whether by describing the purpose of the meetings in a leaflet, which was circulated to those who might join or by talking beforehand to a school class about it, I always made it clear that to attend the group would involve meeting adults who exercised authority in different ways and discovering what could be learned from them. It was this statement which attracted the people who came and in some cases attendance could have been higher had I not restricted the size of the group to twelve. This indicates a strong desire on the part of those young people to interact with and learn from adults as long as a structure was discernible within which meetings would take place. There were few signs of a general hostility to adults nor a desire to attack them at this point; on the contrary there were signs of a strong concern to understand what it means to be an adult, linked with a fear of adults which needed to be coped with realistically.

In testing this in the first meeting with young adults, I normally made a statement about why I wanted to run the group, why their teachers, employers or others wanted the group run and then opened a discussion about what they hoped to get out of it themselves. Their responses always moved around the area of wanting 'to find out about authority' or 'to meet people like policemen and magistrates'. In some cases I met past attenders of groups (on one formal occasion and some informal ones) and it was evident that they all had very clear memories of how various visitors had behaved and what they had learned from them. My opportunity to explore these memories never came less than six months after a group had ended and in some cases was more than a year after it. The clarity of the recall and the impact of the meetings were still evident however long the interval. I recognise problems concerning the collection of this evidence, and that my own presence certainly facilitated the recall, but the point still stands that what was described indicated the value given by the young people to meeting adults — even the ones they had disliked in the sessions.

The behaviour and attitudes here described are generally in agreement with Professor Musgrove's findings in the Midlands about the attitudes of young people to adults and the exercise of authority; they are more favourable than is usually credited. [3]   They also accord with Miss Pearl Jephcott's reports on young people in Glasgow, [4] and the attitudes of young people in further education in London as described by the Eppels. [5]

The dominant impression of the behaviour of these 143 young people, held not only by me but also by many of the visitors they met, has been that they do not in the first instance regard themselves as a species set apart from adults. As one girl of 19 put it, 'I haven't got attitudes about adults — I am an adult'. The majority do not feel at the root of it all that going through the adolescent developmental processes (most of which have taken place physiologically by the time they are 17) makes them fundamentally different from those older than themselves, or sets them apart from adults. In this context it is important to note the comment of Mr E M Eppel:

"It may be worth reflecting that adolescents are people as well as adolescents and that some of the things they do and the conflicts they experience may be as much the consequence of being alive and sentient in a complex and changing social environment as of being in a particular phase of development." [6]

What this means will be further explored in later chapters.

RESPONSES TO THE GROUP METHOD

It has not been possible in the context of this Project to follow up in detail those who attended the groups within it. There are a number of indications that different kinds of changes did take place in those who came, some more important than others. At one level a 15-year old in a school group said at the final session: 'I can now see that people in authority can be helpful, though a lot depends on the person'. A 19-year old printer said: 'I started out before these meetings feeling pretty depressed about things. I am still depressed, but I am not crushed by it now'.

At another level are the indications of how people behaved in settings other than the group itself, indicating some transfer of learning from it. In three of the school groups an examination of the members' attendance records indicated a slight increase in their regularity of attending school while the group was meeting. With the small number of cases and the number of other variables present which could not be identified such a change could not be given much weight as being directly related to the group, though it would be in line with the kind of change hoped for from it. The first group of 10 van-boys taken early in 1967 demonstrated an important change of behaviour. Three months after the group was over all except three were with the same employers. Of those who had left, one had gone to work in his father's restaurant, another had taken a job with training and only one had left for no clearly discernible reason. In the same period the firm had taken on and lost some twenty other young men. In fact two years later four of them were still there, one of them having now become a driver-salesman. The process of identification, which is facilitated by small groups, had helped these boys to find some stability which many of their contemporaries had yet to do.

It is also possible to look at the effect of the group on individuals. The examples given were provided by the probation officer, and the child care officer concerned, and thus have the advantage of some detachment from the process of the groups concerned. Two of the cases were reported in written form to me and represent the officers' interpretations of the situations.

A boy on probation — Billy aged 16[7]

'Billy was placed on probation in November 1967. I (his probation officer) decided from the start that he should attend the group, and that so long as he attended the group, I would play a minimal role, being available only if and when he wanted to see me. I was unsure, but I felt that, since he has a fairly stable home and parents who are concerned about him, I could leave him to work out any difficulties in the group.

'He did see me briefly from time to time though he said little of significance mainly because I did not let him. He talked once of going into the Merchant Navy, but his friend, Sam, had fixed plans for doing this and he may have been influenced by him. Also, talk of going into the Merchant Navy is a common phenomenon amongst boys of his age. He stayed in his job, and the only indication of difficulty centred around the family's accommodation problems; he has to sleep in the same room as his parents. Once in the past there was a row about this and he went off for a time to his sister's in Manchester.

'I deliberately did not visit the home while Billy was attending the group, but in January a crisis blew up and the parents came to see me. The row centred ostensibly at any rate, over Billy's lack of a room, embarrassment at bringing in mates etc. I paid a visit to the home on Friday (Billy was talking of going off to Manchester the following day) and with myself presiding, a grand row developed. His mother cried and said he could leave at once, his father called him various names, and Billy told his parents he didn't care for what they thought. I left feeling I had achieved nothing though I did manage to tell Billy that I would be at my office the following morning. On Saturday Billy left home, but after having come to see me, did not go to Manchester and went round to stay at a mate's. On Sunday he went round to fetch his clothes from home but his parents would not let him have them. Whereupon he went off to the police station, told them what had happened and returned to the house accompanied by a policeman! The upshot was that the policeman talked to both sides and Billy returned home. The parents came to see me on Monday, and with tears and shame that I should have witnessed the scene on Friday, told me of the reconciliation and how helpful the police had been. On Tuesday, Billy came in and his account was similar — 'the policeman straightened it out'.

'My tentative interpretation of all this is as follows: Billy's parents are caring parents but have pretty rigid views. Billy learned from the group, and to a lesser extent from contact with me, that authority can be liberal. I have no direct evidence but I suspect that he may have behaved with his father and mother as he might towards an authority figure in the group; hence, perhaps, the crisis. The interesting thing was that, once the crisis arrived, Billy was able, in the last resort to turn to the police for help. In Hackney, for a young lad to do that is quite an achievement.'

Michael — a boy under supervision by the Children's Department

'Michael, aged $14\frac{1}{2}$, lived with his mother, having spent some six-and-a-half years in the care of the local authority since he was about 7. He had been home for about 15 months when he first attended the group. Before the group started, his mother had found herself very hard put to cope with him. She was a frequent visitor to the Children's Department complaining to me as his child care officer about his foul language and threatening behaviour towards her. His attendance at school during this time was erratic and contributed to her worry.

40

'Michael attended the group for the whole of the three months it ran, his only absences being on occasions when he was away on holiday. Throughout those three months his mother never visited the Department at all and Michael's attendance at school became regular. This pattern was maintained until two months after the ending of the group. At this point his school attendance began to deteriorate again and his mother began to reappear at the office, making the same kind of complaints she had previously.

'As far as was known, there were no other major factors influencing Michael during the periods of his different patterns of behaviour other than his attendance at the group. When he was in the meetings he was reported to be always quiet and withdrawn. A possible interpretation is that the group sessions provided a place in which he was regularly meeting authority figures in a setting which enabled him to work at his conflicts with them, largely inside himself. This freed him from acting out those conflicts in his relationship with his mother and his teachers.

'It is not possible to say for certain whether or not a much longer experience of the group might have achieved a more permanent change in Michael's behaviour though the period of two months after the group during which he stayed fairly stable indicates that it is a reasonable expectation.

A girl under the Children's Department (aged 17)

A further example was quoted orally to me by another child care officer. Following a number of difficult years with a girl, she had the most creative interview she had ever had with her client. Both the officer and the girl attributed the girl's changed attitude and her capacity to make a new relationship to her experience of the small working group. In fact the girl herself reported the incident to me quite independently of her child care officer, but in similar terms.

I recognise that evidence collected in this manner is very unlikely to produce information of a neutral or negative kind and cannot therefore be regarded as appropriate in validly judging the effect of the group. However, it is not my intention here simply to prove the value of the method per se.

The major importance of the group method for the purpose of this Project, has been its function as a research tool to enable study of how relationships between adults and young people are developed. In enabling this to take place what has also happened has been that some young people have derived some significant learning from the experience of meeting a variety of adults in a controlled situation. For the majority of young people most of the time the controls operating in the group are, of course, not present, yet frequently they also derive benefit from meeting adults in their everyday life: the group method seems to have pointed up this experience in some instances and enabled it to be studied.

41

NOTES

(1) Much of the same behaviour was found in the groups met in the Midlands engineering firm before the group method was especially developed.

(2) This probably comes as no surprise to those aware of the findings of the Mothers' Union study 'Do Children Talk to Their Parents?', which uncovered positive feelings for parents on the part of over 2,000 adolescents.

(3)	F Musgrove	Youth and the Social Order especially pp 97-100	Routledge and Kegan Paul 1964
(4)	P Jephcott	Time of One's Own especially pp 88 & 122	Oliver and Boyd 1967
(5)	E M and M Eppel	Adolescents and Morality	Routledge and Kegan Paul 1966
(6)	E M Eppel	The Adolescent Predicament. Lecture to the Annual Conference of the National Association for Mental Health, 1967	NAMH 1967

(7) The names are fictitious, though all cases are real.

4. The Behaviour of Adults in the Groups

A continually significant factor in understanding the behaviour of young people in the groups has been the behaviour of the adults who have been present. I have already drawn some attention to this, mentioning how my own occasional absences affected the attendance at subsequent sessions of a group, and also how some of the visitors influenced the behaviour of members. During the last fourteen months of the Project I paid special attention to the examination of this aspect. In order to do this I spent periods of up to four hours with visitors before they came to a group and similar periods of time after they attended. By doing this I was able to examine visitors' feelings and anticipations prior to the group, their behaviour in it and their reflections upon their visit. At the same time I was in a position to examine the developing life of the group of young people. In this way each meeting could be looked at as an intersection of two lines of development, both of which I was observing.

Following the description of the small working-group method, I outlined five incidents from different groups. Each of these gives some indication of the relationship between the behaviour of the young people and that of the visitor; each illustrates something different but for a fuller exploration of this area it is necessary to describe one session in much greater detail.

An example

Five boys aged 16 and 17 were present at a session to meet a priest. They were all employees at the same firm, working as van-boys or junior warehousemen, and had been meeting as a group for three-and-a-half months. At that particular point in time they were feeling both angry and anxious about the situation in which they found themselves. Three weeks earlier a 'mate' of theirs had been dismissed in circumstances which they felt to be unfair. They were anxious because they realised that they might easily find themselves in similar circumstances, and they had no wish to lose their own jobs. The two most recent visitors to their sessions had been a trades unionist and an employer, both of whom (despite what might have been expected from their roles) had quite failed to help the boys work at the problem they presented. This was because neither of them had been able to cope with the strength of the boys' feelings about this issue and had tended to play the whole thing down and to minimise it. This meant that the boys who came to the session to meet the priest were full of unresolved feelings from earlier meetings. In fact they had expressed the opinion that a priest had very little to offer them at this point in time anyway. The group as a whole showed their feelings on this through their attendance at the session; nine had attended the visit of the trades unionist and six that of the employer, now only five were present. Those who came sat around the priest and myself, lolling listlessly in their chairs and muttering to each other. I had some remarks about the series as a whole I wished to make, as well as making a brief introduction of the visitor. As I spoke I felt that I was largely being ignored and that the boys were by now very angry indeed. Finally, having introduced the priest to the boys, and them to him, I handed over to him; by now I was expecting a difficult and maybe painful session.

He spoke for a few moments, saying that he had been in commerce before he had become a priest and, having completed his time as a curate, he was now in charge of one of the local parish churches. He then invited any questions. The boys shifted in their chairs for a moment looking between each other to see who would speak first. The oldest of them, who had until then been sitting almost completely turned around in his chair so that he presented his back to the visitor, faced the priest and said 'So why did you become a priest then?' 'Because God wanted me to' came the immediate reply. I could feel a shock go round the group; I could also feel the way the priest was now exposed to them. He had laid himself open to their derision and scepticism. He did not develop or cover up what he had said, nor did he attempt any explanations. He simply behaved in a way that showed that he felt he had answered the question put to him. The boys began to sit up and look at him; they were still angry and sceptical about what he had to offer them. 'How did you know God wanted you to do that?' 'It wasn't really a voice speaking to me, in the ordinary way we talk to one another and tell each other things' he said, 'It was more that the things which happened to me, and the feelings I had all added up to my realising that God was telling me to become a minister. I prefer to call myself a minister rather than a priest'. By now the boys were facing him, ready to take things up with him. The discussion began to get under way; the questions ranged around what a minister did besides 'praying and preaching at people to be good', what did he think about death and marriage; what was baptism for; was he afraid of dying? As his answers emerged and he developed and shared them with the boys it was clear that he had a fairly fundamentalist approach; he said on many occasions

'The Bible tells me....' and 'Jesus said this so that is good enough for me'. But it was also clear that these were not things which he was using to be defensive but rather, enabled him to lay himself wide open to different kinds of situation. The boys tested him on this when they were talking about the effect of prayer. He gave an example from his experience the day before, when a woman on drugs had been referred to him by a doctor who had failed to help her. She was not a churchgoer herself. He had talked with her about her problem, had prayed with her and finally laid his hands upon her. Before she left he had asked her to give him the tablets she was on and he had proceeded to throw them away. 'You will not need them any more, the Holy Spirit will take care of you now' he had said to her. 'I shall see her next week' he said to the boys ' and she will be cured'. They looked at him, stunned both by his certainty and the risk of failure to which he was committing himself, made worse by telling them about it even before he knew the final outcome of the incident.

As the session developed the behaviour of the five boys steadily changed; more of them spoke than in previous sessions; they spoke seriously of their own experiences, of religious instruction in schools, going to church, of their feelings about death. I drew attention to how differently they were behaving in comparison with other earlier sessions, particularly the two most recent ones. I pointed out that there seemed to be a greater feeling of freedom around, people were able to agree and to disagree without falling silent or being pushed into more extreme positions than they may wish to take up.

When the meeting was over they walked off down the street talking to the minister, and when I left about five minutes later I found that two of them had come back to tell me that this had been the best session they had had. 'You could really talk to him' they said, 'he really answered our questions'. As I reflected on this I noted that on many issues they had disagreed with him, on others they had not really understood the content of what he had said, but I also noted that there was a quality in the relationship which he had established which gave value to their point of view and their feelings, yet which never denied his own, particularly his feelings about his relationship with God.

ASPECTS OF THE BEHAVIOUR OF ADULTS
OBSERVED TO BE SUPPORTIVE TO GROUP MEMBERS

This example draws out a number of important features of what may be considered as behaviour which was experienced by young people as supportive.

TOLERATING UNCERTAINTY

The first, and possibly the most important feature was that this visitor was able to tolerate uncertainty. Time and again he behaved in a way which meant that, though he knew the point from which he was stepping, he could not be certain what would be the outcome of what he said or did; he trusted himself to others present, expecting them to work with what he had contributed and to take it further. This is a point which has been well described by William James in a letter to his wife on when a man's 'character' is discernible: moments at which 'there is a voice inside which says "This is the real me!" ' He goes on to say that such experience always includes '... an element of active tension, of holding my own as it were, and trusting outward things to perform their part so as to make it a full harmony, but without any guaranty that they will. .... Make it a guaranty and the attitude immediately becomes to my consciousness stagnant and stingless'. [1]

In order for this visiting priest to be able to behave in this way in relation to the young employees he was meeting, he needed to be convinced about what was real in himself and in his past experience. His reply to the first question, about his becoming a priest, made this plain to those present, not simply by the words he used but because at the moment of making the reply one was aware of an insight into the depths of him as a person; there were no defences apparent, despite the obvious hostility of his questioners at the time. This meant that the experience of all present, the young men, myself and the priest was a wholly **new** experience because none of us could be certain what would come next.

By behaving thus, he gave the members of the group freedom to approach what he had to say in their own way; to treat it cynically, to explore it, to express approval or anything else they wished. There was a considerable amount of tension present throughout the session: not a tension arising from fear but from straining to understand and to learn. In the model of his own behaviour the visitor demonstrated how to respond to that self-same tension and use it constructively. Intuitively the young men recognised this; it is worth noting that none of the five missed another session throughout the rest of the series, with the exception of one who was accepted to work in the Post Office and left to take this up before the end of the series. Three others who were not present at this session continued to attend sporadically to the end.

THE RECOGNITION OF OTHER RELATIONSHIPS

A second point, connected with the capacity to tolerate uncertainty, is also apparent in this example. Part of the reality of each person is the relationships in which he is involved, in other words the persons from whom he has introjected parts to make up his own personality. Where a person is under stress he draws on these other relationships to help him cope with that stress. The problem for each person is to recognise and distinguish the relationships which are significant to one in a situation and from them to draw on those which are relevant to it. In the example given, the priest constantly drew

46

attention to his relationship with God through Christ and invited the young men to explore and test this relationship if they wished to do so, particularly in his reply to that first question. Other instances have occurred in other groups; for example an employer visiting a group of students at a college of further education started out by saying 'In the first instance, as an employer I must make sure that the profit the firm makes for its shareholders gives them a reasonable return on their capital invested in the company. If I fail to do that, the whole thing will go bust or be taken over and my employees will be likely to lose their jobs'. By so doing he drew attention to his relationships with both those to whom he was accountable and those for whom he was responsible. The group then took these up and explored how he coped with the tensions which were inevitably involved.

A problem exists for those who belong to a group which arouses hostility in young people because one finds oneself being asked to take responsibility for the actions of those seen as colleagues. On one occasion a prison officer was visiting a group at a youth club, a group which included two boys who had done spells in detention centres. Both were complaining bitterly about the unreasonableness of 'the screws' and one cited as an example having been given two minutes in which to have a bath including getting undressed, bathed and getting dressed again. The visitor immediately responded as if the resented instruction had been given in his own establishment and said, 'I expect you had been causing a bit of bother in the bathroom on a previous occasion and deserved to be made to hurry that time'. The boy agreed that this was the case. By taking the issue up in this way, the prison officer demonstrated that he accepted responsibility for believing that the action of his colleague was reasonable even though he was not present himself nor did he know the officer in question. He thus acknowledged his professional relationship and gave those present the opportunity to examine this further.

To do this is not necessarily easy, particularly where the examples which a group quoted to a visitor are about failure of one kind or another, the corrupt policeman, the bullying prison officer, or the callous doctor or nurse. Adult behaviour in dealing with such instances has involved exploring the actual facts of an incident in order to get at what is really being presented, and then to try to explore it and its problems from the point of view of one's own feelings and knowledge. For example, a police sergeant was questioned on what was seen to be unnecessary roughness in handling spectators at a football match. He got the details of a specific instance from the group and then described his own feelings about having to dive into a seething crowd at a point where trouble is obviously breaking out, the panic at being vastly outnumbered, the difficulty of identifying the real troublemakers and the need to act decisively if the situation is not to get out of hand. He admitted that mistakes are made, people are handled roughly and the wrong people sometimes get taken, not simply because of mistaken identity but often because the policeman concerned feels that he must get out of an overwhelming situation yet must also be seen to have achieved something. The sergeant went on to talk of the difficulty which such actions presented him as supervising officer when his subordinates behaved in this way.

In all these instances each individual visitor, having been invited to a group in his role as a priest, an employer, a prison officer and a policeman drew attention to relationships which were both real and relevant to the role in which they came to the group. Though they also had other real relationships such as with their wives and families they did not draw these into the discussion except in so far as they affected or were influenced by the role taken by the visitor in the group. For example, a senior officer in the Fire Service talked of how working a regular 96 hour week caused him to have an unusual kind of family life; in this instance he referred to his relationship with his wife and daughter in a way relevant to his role in the group as a representative of the Service.

The effect of taking account of and drawing attention to these relationships was to enable members of groups to recognise, not simply an individual in front of them, but the focus of a whole series of relationships. This enabled them to be able better to focus their own view of the visitor, often because of their own memories of dealing with his colleagues, and to work out how to establish their relationship with him in the 'here and now'. This gave them a sense of security when in contact with such a person since it got rid of unnecessary uncertainties about the visitor, thus making it easier to make constructive use of whatever he offered them. It helped them to understand the nature of their own authority in the immediate situation, and it also gave them some sense of being in a real relationship with the wider community represented to them by the visitor.

ACKNOWLEDGING DIFFICULTIES

A different feature in the behaviour of visiting adults was a capacity to be frank about difficulties. This included acknowledging difficulties in the 'back-home' situation, as was the case with the police sergeant given already, but it also applied to the 'here and now' of the actual meeting. A young prison officer meeting a group of boys in their last term at school, was puzzled and concerned at the way they were behaving towards him. They muttered to each other and took very little notice of anything he said. At last he burst out, 'I've met a lot of lads before, but I've never met a bunch like you. Why did you ask me along if you don't want to talk with me?' The boys were stunned for a moment but as they recovered they began to be able to talk to the visitor, to question him and comment on his answers. As they left at the end of the session, one of them (who had a brother in prison) said sheepishly, 'Sorry we was like we was'. Or again, a probation officer was trying to help a group of young printers understand what his role was. They were having great difficulty in holding the punitive and supportive parts of his job together. In fact they were failing to do this. Realising that they had met a prison officer the week before, he told them that a probation officer's job was more complicated to understand because it was less clearly defined than a prison officer's. He went on to say that this meant that both a probation officer and those who met him probably had to work much harder at understanding things if they were to get anything out of their meeting. This was a comment which could be taken as referring to the immediate situation as well as his ordinary work place. It was the turning point of that particular session; all sorts of issues were then able to be raised by the young men and half-an-hour later it was hard to bring the meeting to a close on time.

It is worth making the point that in both these instances the difficulty which the visitors faced was described by both of them in a way which enabled the whole group to acknowledge the problem as a concern which was shared by them all. What was real to each visitor was the capacity to face the difficulty and try to work at it, thus helping the group to recognise that reality and to work at it themselves.

THE RECOGNITION OF WHAT IS REAL IN OTHERS

It is apparent that visitors to the groups frequently found it very hard to recognise the reality of the experience and situation of the particular young people they met. Partly this was due to preconceptions about young people being carried into a session, which then influenced a visitor's behaviour more than did the questions he was asked or the way he was treated by those present. It was also partly due to a failure to realise that many of the problems experienced by a young adult are remarkably similar to those which puzzle people about thirty years older.

In the example of the priest, one of the issues which was explored at some length was the question of death. In the discussion the young men were able to talk openly about their own feelings and fears on this issue and to hear what the visitor felt and believed about this. Because the young men spoke openly it was possible to see what was real about death for them without making assumptions about their views which might not be warranted. [2] This required two important things. The first was a capacity to listen to what the young people were actually saying, not only to hear the words used but also to recognise the feelings which were being expressed at the time. The second was a capacity to wait in silence and allow a group to think about what they wanted to say and how they wanted to say it. In this way it was possible for a visitor to begin to recognise what was itself adult in the responses offered by others; he could then take this up and work on it with the group.

Linked with this was the importance a visitor attached to getting at the truth of what members of a group thought and felt about an issue, including what they felt about themselves and about him. There were many occasions on which there were inconsistencies in the way an incident was described or feelings were talked about. It was often tempting to accept these without question yet to do so would have been to avoid discovering what was real. For example, some young people would describe their own behaviour in certain instances in almost ludicrously glowing terms which they knew to be untrue. A girl of 15 who attended a group run as part of the preventive work of a Children's Department, began by giving one visitor the impression that she never stayed out after 10.0 pm at night. The truth was that she had come home during the early hours of the morning on many occasions and sometimes been out for whole nights. By the end of the session she was admitting to having returned home at 2.0 am the previous night. It was then possible for the visitor to talk from his experience as a father with a daughter who had herself spent some nights out. By helping to reach a more realistic presentation of herself it was possible to demonstrate that what was real was not so terrible that it must be deliberately hidden by lies. In other words her real self was given a value by the visitor in a way she had not done in her own estimation. To have accepted her original descriptions unquestioningly would have been to collude with her devaluation of herself.

On other occasions young people have described incidents in a way which included inconsistencies of which they were not immediately aware but which enabled over-simplified views of a situation to be held. A probation officer was meeting a group of young school leavers and the discussion ranged round the law, the importance of punishment for wrong-doing (which the group rated very highly) and then the iniquity of the police. The point was reached where they were beginning to say that it would be better not to have a police force at all. The probation officer here cut in saying 'It's a funny thing, because you have been saying that people should be punished for what they do wrong. Those who are going to be punished have got to be caught so there must be someone to do the catching'. There was a moment of silence — then a boy said 'Yer, but it's the way they catch 'em'.

The probation officer's remark had helped focus attention on what was the real problem which concerned the group (which was the behaviour of some policemen), and had cut away the distortion which had led to the inconsistency of the position they had taken up.

An interesting point about the importance of recognising what is real in others is made by the 10th century philosopher Kahlil Gibran:

"No man can reveal to you ought but that which already lies asleep
in the dawning of your knowledge. If he is indeed wise he does not
bid you enter the house of his wisdom but rather leads you to the
threshold of your own mind." (3)

VISITORS' PERCEPTION OF THE PROJECT OFFICER

One part of the reality of the situation in which these visitors found themselves was my own presence in the group, and their own behaviour was
affected by how they saw me. This was a point of some difficulty to a number of them. Where they saw my function as being to provide opportunities
for the young people to learn and interpreted my behaviour in this light, then
they found little difficulty in working with the group. This is an area of some
significance since it concerns how the relationship between two adults influenced the behaviour of the young people; this will be returned to later on and
discussed in more detail. The important point to make here, was that those
visitors who displayed adult behaviour in relation to my presence in the group
were those who were able to perceive the meeting as having a unity which included me, rather than looking on it as a number of disjointed and unconnected
parts — myself, the young people and the visitor.

To some extent what has been said in this section can be summarised by
saying that adult behaviour required a capacity to recognise and respond to
what was real in the behaviour and experience of those present. If the behaviour
was immature, as in the incident of the schoolboys and the prison officer, it
was important that this was recognised and responded to in a way which
showed that it had been recognised. It would have been destructive to pretend that their behaviour was otherwise, just as the girl who stayed out late
would not have been helped by pretending she was as faultless as she wanted
to make out. Wherever the behaviour and attitudes of the young people showed
maturity, that in its turn needed to be given value and worked with.

RECOGNITION OF APPROPRIATE RELATIONSHIPS

There is no doubt that those who come to these small working groups as
visitors had agreed to do something which was difficult. They were being
invited in as the representatives of all those who took the same role in society.
They were also, inevitably, representatives of other adults. They were not
asked to give a lecture but to offer their experience as a resource to help
the members of groups explore what it means to be an adult in society. Thus
they were coming in not simply to show what, say, a doctor or a fireman
does, but to discuss what it feels like to deal with those who are sick, and
to take personal risks to save property and persons from fire. They were
asked to work for ninety minutes on the basis of the questions which the members of the group put to them, not to direct the conversation themselves except in so far as it was important to clarify an issue already raised. They
were asked to recognise that decisions about what would be discussed and in
what way, lay basically with the young people, and that they must resist any
temptation they might feel to take the session over and run it in a way which

might be more satisfying to themselves. It was pointed out that frequently a period of silence could be very constructive in the development of a session. Visitors were warned that they may not always find the issues they were asked about very easy to deal with but that the most complicated aspects might in the long run have the most creative value for a session, if they could be worked at.

Thus the relationship between visitor and group was between one offering a resource in terms of **his** own experience and those who wished to use it to help understand **their** own experience. It involved recognising the nature of leadership appropriate to the role of the group members and the nature of leadership appropriate to the visitor's role and seeing the complementary nature of these. Part of my role entailed behaving in a way which helped the others to define their roles, thus enabling them to work together; it was important for a visitor to be able to perceive this.

The example given of the priest illustrates clearly how one visitor behaved appropriately in relation to the task of the group. One way of describing this is to say that the group was able to work 'through' him, as was demonstrated by their subsequent comment about him 'really answering' their questions. The prison officer who was ignored, also behaved appropriately because he drew attention to this role and to the failure of the boys to fulfil the role they were committed to by inviting him to be present at the meeting.

The same was true of the probation officer who commented on the difficulty of understanding his own role which demanded work of those who met him. He was showing that he recognised his dependence upon their capacity to grapple with the difficulty if he wished to help them understand.

The question of appropriate relationships between the visitor, the group and myself can be put another way by saying that what was particularly called for was a realistic recognition of the nature of the dependence each had upon others in their particular situation and a capacity to work with this, whatever shortcomings and anxieties might arise.

THE RESPONSES OF YOUNG PEOPLE TO THESE KINDS OF BEHAVIOUR

The consistent response of the members of groups to these kinds of behaviour on the part of visitors, was an attempt to call forth from themselves behaviour of the same kind. It was not necessarily immediate, as was evident when the van-boys were faced with the priest's reply to their first question, nor was it necessarily maintained for the whole of the rest of a session, particularly if a visitor was not himself able to keep it up.

A policeman visited a group of young printers. They were aged between 15 and 18 and found it difficult to work out how to talk with him. Two of them talked of their own past behaviour which had involved breaking the law, though they had not been caught. The same two went on to talk about 'feeling sick' when they heard of illegal activity by policemen. This meant that a discussion ensued about the problem of people using the police to do all the controlling of certain kinds of behaviour, leaving everyone else to feel free to do what they like, yet hating the police both when they caught them for an offence and when policemen failed to live up to what was expected of them. The unreality of this situation was soon apparent and it was then possible to draw a parallel between what had been discussed, the conclusions they had drawn and the way their own behaviour in the session had changed. They felt that they hated policemen but were finding it hard to hate this one. They put pressure on him to get him either to behave brutally and so confirm their expectations or to be so 'nice' and different from all other constables that they could say 'He wasn't a proper policeman'. He resisted both pressures as he talked about his work; he described the problem of using his discretion about how to deal with different kinds of offences, pointing out that his decision about whether or not to charge someone was the first step in taking an offender to court. As he talked in this vein, showing something of what it is like to be a policeman, the young men began to open up. They talked of their feelings about 'bent coppers', and from an unrealistic view of the police which had almost paralysed them in the early part of the session, they moved on to an understanding which enabled them to feel free to explore the truth with the visitor.

It was very seldom that a consistent attempt by a visitor to maintain his behaviour at this sort of level was overridden by the immature behaviour of the members of a group. The few occasions where it did occur, were all in groups of young people in their last year at school, where the group met as part of the school's curriculum of social or general studies.

Where a visitor could tolerate stress and uncertainty in exploring an issue, so also could the young people; where he demonstrated a concern to get at the truth of an incident, so also did the members of the group; where a visitor showed that he was not afraid of being disagreed with or even attacked for what he represented, then the conflict which arose could be used creatively (this included the exploration of differences between the visitor and myself); where a visitor was not paralysed by his own mishandling of a situation but was able to work through its effects as the session went on, the young people were able to recover themselves with him. An example of this latter was the occasion on which an Army NCO visited the same van-boys and warehousemen who met the priest. He began the session very nervous and defensive. He answered questions about his service brusquely and without giving anything away; the boys grew restive and angry because they felt he was in some way depriving them. Seeing how the session was developing I asked the visitor about his medal ribbons, believing that if he could talk about these and what they meant to him he might be able to re-establish himself. Quietly and shyly he talked about them including the personal decorations

53

which he wore as well as the campaign ribbons. He talked awkwardly, obviously frightened of seeming to boast, but as he grappled with his feelings, the boys began to appreciate his problem. They thought more carefully as they phrased further questions and comments. At the end, the relationship established between them was one which contained elements of interest and respect for each other; in fact the boys decided to extend the session by ten minutes to discuss the need for an army in peacetime, despite the fact that they were all planning to watch Arsenal play West Bromwich Albion at Highbury and to extend the session meant running some risk of not being able to get in.

MY OWN RESPONSE TO SUCH BEHAVIOUR

From my own point of view, I found that where a visitor behaved in this way I was able to describe the issues arising in a session and make comments which went beyond the immediate situation of those present in the room and took account of other situations such as the firm for which the group worked, their homes and families and wider implications for other parts of society. The important point was that such contributions could be rooted in the 'here and now' behaviour of the group and extrapolated outwards without seeming to be punitive, but rather to facilitate insight. This meant that the groups could use what I was offering to some constructive effect.

It was evident that what was communicated by supportive behaviour such as has been described in this chapter was not simply something to do with a visitor's personality. It was more a quality communicated through that person's behaviour which spread into the relationships he or she established and which affected and was taken up by those encountered. It seemed to call forth similar behaviour in the young people in the groups and also in myself. In the second paragraph on page 51 I have indicated that this quality could be referred to as 'adult behaviour'. In Chapter 7 this will be explored further, but at this point it is important to underline the importance of such behaviour in helping young people take up full adult roles in a constructive way because it enabled them to find from within themselves what was real and what was needed by the situation. Yet it was not simply a question of finding what was real inside themselves, but also because what was real in the world around was able to be experienced by them at the same time, because others present drew attention to it. The whole situation was thus a reciprocal one and the contribution of the visitor, because so much attention was inevitably focused upon him, was the key to it all.

There is one final point to be made, a point which in some ways emerges as surprising, yet is also extremely important. In a reading of this chapter it will have been evident that many of the examples have been drawn from visitors who are concerned with the maintenance of law and order — even more, a high proportion of those have actually attended the groups in uniform. It is worth adding that they were not all necessarily liked and their various agencies did not necessarily rise in the estimation of the young adults. Yet the fact was that it was these people who created more opportunities for the members of groups to respond in adult ways than were created by teachers, social workers, priests and elected representatives. This is not to say that the latter could not (there are examples quoted here to show that some did), but they did not create or recognise the same opportunities as frequently as most of the policemen, prison officers and magistrates. This will be explored further in the next chapter.

NOTES

(1) Henry James   The Letters of William James   Faber and Faber 1967
quoted in 'Identity, Youth in
Crisis (Erikson) p 19

(2) It is worth noting that all the groups who asked to meet a priest (four in all) raised the question of death with the visitor.

(3) Quoted by   Discussion Leading and Group   Iliffe 1968
J W Barber   Training Techniques —
Industrial Training Handbook
(Ed) J W Barber

5. The Defences of Visiting Adults

FACTORS MAKING FOR STRESS – FEAR OF YOUNG PEOPLE

Not all the adults who have visited groups have been able to maintain a pattern of the kind of behaviour described; few, including myself, have been able to sustain it for ninety minutes. Many have achieved it on some occasions, a few others have never achieved it at all. The main problem was that adults frequently felt as if the young people wished in some way or other to attack them. This seldom related to the actual behaviour of those they met. There was a fear of being exposed, of being found inadequate and, at least in an imaginary way, being destroyed by the young people present. It was evident from the discussion I had with visitors before they came to a session that they were apprehensive, yet often found difficulty in voicing what their apprehension was about. For example, it was apparent that a police sergeant preparing to meet a group of students on day-release from the Civil Service equated them in his mind with demonstrators in the Grosvenor Square riots of March 1968; a doctor preparing to meet a group of young workers wanted to bring his son with him ('He has long hair and is keen on the Beatles') to show that 'a bridge can be made between the generations.' The odd thing was that he did not recognise their invitation to him showed that they already believed that such a bridge could be made. Many of the visitors assumed, usually without evidence, that the members of the group they were going to visit were suffering from personality disorders which would cause them to be very aggressive. When it was clear to me that these sorts of expectations were likely to affect how a visitor would behave in the group, I would articulate this to them, pointing out the impression I had picked up of their views of the young people they would be meeting. Though these were often denied, in the stress of the actual situation there were many occasions when the same attitudes would reappear and affect what went on. It is difficult to pin down accurately the reason for visiting adults' fear of exposure. It might have been that they actually perceived themselves in a way they hoped others would not perceive them, that is as being fragile; or it may have been that however a visitor perceived himself, he believed that young people would perceive him in a way which would cause them to want to attack. The evidence of this Project suggests the former, as will be apparent in this and later chapters.

FEAR OF FAILURE AND UNCERTAINTY

Another factor making for stress was the frequent unconscious expectation in the young people that adults should not fail or be uncertain. This unspoken expectation was picked up by a visitor and, given his own needs to feel successful and sure about things, would be colluded with. This meant denying the existence of such feelings as uncertainty and the possibility of failure, or of finding a way to avoid them and thus to avoid the anticipated anger at not having lived up to expectations. The anxiety about this was certainly made more problematical for visitors by the fact that I was present in the meeting and they could have no guarantee that I would cover up difficulties for them nor even allow them to do it for themselves. A visitor thus might feel caught between the expectations of the group, his own needs to appear successful and admired, and his expectations of how I would react. Inevitably this made for stress.

Over and above all this, the sheer business which they were asked to help with was itself complicated; involving exposure and difficulty, let alone taking into account what has just been said.

WAYS OF COPING WITH STRESS

It is not surprising therefore that different ways were sought by visitors to help cope with the stress they experienced or anticipated, ways which protected them from making real contact with the members of the groups and resulted in the destruction of opportunities for young people in the situation to experience that moment of saying 'This is the real me', and 'This is the real world'.

TOTAL CONTROL OR TOTAL ABDICATION

A number of different kinds of defences were used by visitors to protect themselves. Some of these have been attempts to control the external situation, others to control the person's own inner world. These can be examined as points on a continuum between those visitors who attempted to maintain total control of the situation and those who totally abdicated. Illustrations of the two extremes were (i) a man who told an almost continual stream of stories about his life in the world of sport, including recounting his 'most embarrassing moment' and explaining why he was now wearing white socks, and (ii) a person who was lost after a few minutes and who sat there whispering to me 'I don't know what to do' while in front of us the group disintegrated and its members went in and out of the room on what they euphemistically

57

called 'visits to the lavatory'. In both these instances I found myself completely caught up in the process which was taking place and was only sporadically able to try doing anything which might have any value.

There were only a few occasions on which either of these two extremes was reached. Much more frequently control of the situation was shared between those present, but certain devices were used to prevent the full exploration of anyone's experience, thus attempting to ensure that the balance of control lay with the visitor. The common basis of these devices was tacitly to redefine the task of the meeting so that what was offered for exploration entailed tolerating only the minimum level of anxiety which the visitor wanted. Examples of this occurred whenever a visitor took the initiative and began to ask the group what they thought of different matters and how young people felt about this or that issue.

DENIAL OF ROLE

Some visitors, having come to a group, would talk about experience in roles other than the one they were invited to explore with the group. Generally what was done was to move from a role in which a visitor felt uncertain about some aspects (or even all of it) to a role in which he had more confidence. One man was invited to a group to talk about being a magistrate; he was an attractive and amusing person with a wide variety of interests and experiences He began not by giving an introduction of himself, but by asking the group what experience they had of being in court. Finding that only one of them had, and that a long time ago, he showed some sense of disappointment. It seemed that he had hoped to be faced with vehement criticisms of injustice phrased so immoderately that he could counter them quite easily. In this way the responsibility for the initiative could be placed with the boys, but in a way which left them exposed and himself defended. Instead it was apparent that he would now have to talk about his real experience and allow the group to respond to that. Clearly this placed him in a different position because it involved committing himself to a point of view before he knew how the group would respond to what he felt. He appeared reluctant to do this: instead he manoeuvred the discussion round to questions of social class, through questions of class to the life of his own family and his role as a parent. What he had to say about this was of interest to the group and they behaved in a lively fashion with him.

The significant thing was that the visitor had subtly changed the role he was in from that of magistrate to that of parent, and the message left with the group, though they were not fully aware of it till the session was over, was that they could not trust a visitor to do what he was asked to do, even though they had enjoyed what he had done at the time.

The effect of this was to make the members of that group much more wary of visitors in the next few sessions, avoiding taking risks with them and avoiding exploring issues which really mattered. In other words, they regressed to a more immature pattern of behaviour than they were capable of displaying and were often unnecessarily defensive on subsequent occasions. In terms of adult behaviour, what was avoided here was an exploration of how this person coped with difficult issues which he was not easily able to escape. What he gave was a model of avoidance at the cost of being dependable.

Another form of this denial of role was to split one's role up into parts and to behave as if they were unconnected, to seem to be one person in one situation and a quite different one in another. A prison officer talking about his experience of working in a borstal made it seem as if he behaved as a kind of automaton when he was on duty, not being really responsible for his actions at such times, but when he was off duty and playing table tennis with the boys, he became a 'real' person. He made it clear in the group that he resented being asked to come in uniform because it stopped him feeling free to talk as he wanted to. In the end however, when he had a chance to reflect on the behaviour of the young men and women present, he did accept that it had helped the group to see him more clearly.

A variation of this splitting could also occur when a visitor implied that his behaviour in the group was different from his behaviour elsewhere, usually implying that he could be a 'real' person here, which he could not be elsewhere. Sometimes this was built up by a visitor in such a way that all one could be aware of was so personalised that any task, role or structure became lost. One felt that one was meeting some colossus who seemed to exist quite separately from anything else. On many occasions such a visitor was able to capture a group completely and the young people (and sometimes myself) became spellbound by him, quite swallowed up in his description of himself and the things about him. Problems disappeared as if by magic and the feeling arose that with such a person around all things were possible. But in the end all group members had to go back to their own lives and live these, unhelped by the experience of meeting this person. Such visitors as this usually left the young people more depressed and more frustrated than when they started. By denying their role, including their role as defined in the group and their role in society, thus ignoring reality, such visitors offered nothing to help young adults in their development beyond an hour or so's dream with someone who was not real at that time because he had not explored the truth about adult life with them at all.

THE USE OF PROFESSIONAL SKILLS AS A DEFENCE

A defence used by a number of visitors was to behave as if the group meetings were their own working situation. This is really a different form of the pattern just described, though here the professional role was established in a way which obliterated the visitor's role in the group. It enabled a display of professional skill, but did not enable an exploration of the personal feelings involved in using such skill. To put this another way, what was being offered was simply a role not a view of what it means to be a person taking a role. This might have had some value to anyone wishing to learn particular skills, but was of little value to those who wished to find out something about adulthood.

A child care officer was visiting a group meeting in a youth club. At first she had to clear up certain confusions which some of the group had about her being a health visitor and helping people learn how to feed and care for babies. Then one of the boys present began to raise some problems which he had experienced with a child care officer from another borough. He had got his 15-year-old girl friend pregnant. She was under the supervision of a Children's Department and the CCO's advice to the parents had been to make the girl break off the relationship. The young man had found himself prevented from seeing his girl friend, whom he now wanted to marry. He had tried to see her at her home, but her father had got the police to remove him. He had then gone to the Children's Department to talk to the CCO and had been removed again. The whole experience had been extremely painful to him and he felt that at no point had his feelings been really taken into consideration though he had made them plain. He wanted to know why. The CCO in the meeting treated his story as if it were a case presented to her at work. She asked him questions to get more information. It seemed as if they were the only two people present; this ignored the fact that five others including myself and an adult observer were sitting round the same table. After twenty minutes or so she had assembled a very clear picture of the incident and she had done it quite skilfully. But she never answered his question about why he had been treated as he had nor did she indicate what her own feelings were like in similar instances. What she said was that all CCOs were different and she could not answer for her colleagues, particularly one she did not know.

In discussion with her afterwards I asked how she had felt about the session and she said that it had been very similar to her ordinary working situation. This was confirmation that she had been using her professional skills defensively, rather than allowing the members of the group to explore her experience as an adult and learn from it.

In another instance, a doctor was asked about dealing with depression, particularly when it arose from finding oneself in a situation from which there was no apparent way out. He began by saying that he never encountered this himself because there were always specialists to whom he could pass the problem. The members of the group pressed him further about how they could deal with depression as they experienced it, whereupon he selected one of them and conducted a public consultation with him. In fact, this only caused the group to feel increasingly frustrated and the session actually ended in greater depression than it had opened. On leaving, the doctor commented to me that though he had found the session interesting he felt that I was taking a sledge-hammer to crack a nut. This in turn left me even more angry and depressed by his failure to understand what he had done, and my own incapacity to do anything about it.

I realised as we parted that one problem from which a doctor has no way out occurs when he has to cope with a patient he knows to be dying; but we had not explored that in the session. We had avoided looking at the one issue which might have been the most helpful we could have explored. It came as only a slight surprise when I heard later that the boy on whom the 'consultation' had been carried out, was ill and absent from work for three days following the meeting.

Those visitors who were used to working with young people were most susceptible to defending themselves in this way. At a superficial level it is obvious that a reason for this was that to be surrounded by young people in a setting reminiscent of a discussion group called forth responses of a familiar kind in say, a teacher, or a school psychologist. But at another level, there are three points which need noting. One was the failure to appreciate the task of these particular meetings as being different from other discussion groups, (each of which may well have been quite different from each other). Secondly, I have said that the professional skills were used defensively. This indicated that there was something felt to be inherently dangerous in an adult meeting a group of young people, particularly those who left school at 15. This was an attitude held and affecting a person's behaviour, probably unconsciously, even by those who work regularly with them. This relates to the third point, and raises the question of the extent to which teachers, youth leaders and others are aware of the occasions on which they defend themselves against exploration by young adults and when they are aware of having given freedom for such an exploration to take place. The experience of these visitors indicates that such are largely unaware of this issue. In other words, what appeared to be intuitive behaviour prevented young people learning what it meant to be adult and because it was so obviously intuitive it may well occur elsewhere in schools and in clubs.

ATTEMPTS TO CHANGE THE ROLE OF MEMBERS OF THE GROUP

In many ways the pattern of defences just described was linked with attempts to make the members of the group change role. The CCO and the doctor attempted to turn the members of the group into clients or patients, when they were neither. Others behaved towards the young people in ways which rein-forced feelings of being young, inexperienced and ignorant, feelings which had some reality to them, but which were magnified at the expense of what experience was real to them and what things they did know about. This could be done in a variety of ways, for instance, saying, after a silence, 'Why

61

don't you ask me about ...' or 'I often get asked about ...'.

Another way, which had the effect of identifying the members of the group with all other young people, rather than taking account of the special features of this particular group, was to say 'I have often wanted to know what young people think about ...'. Or again a visitor could significantly affect how the members of a group behaved by taking the initiative from them and questioning them about their experience. One teacher did this with a group of young employees and after a few moments had even asked those who had enjoyed school to put their hands up! To give him credit, he did realise what he had done after he had done it.

A number of visitors had difficulty in relating to the whole group they met, selecting one or two members through whom discussion proceeded without taking account of what other people were doing. In two or three cases this reached the point where those not engaged with the visitor reached the point of actually hitting each other, without any notice seeming to be taken of them. Sometimes a visitor would behave as an attractive woman borough councillor did, which was to engage each of the young men present in a series of individual discussions which resulted in their vying for her favours rather than working with her as a group and learning together of her real experience as a borough councillor. On the other hand, though they were aware of her as a woman, she did not help them really explore any questions of sexuality because the content of her discussion was to do with local politics.

THE DEFENSIVE USE OF A VISITOR'S RELATIONSHIP WITH ME

I met all the visitors for some time before they came to the group. In some cases I spent up to four hours with a prospective visitor. The reasons for this were concerned with the development of the research side of the Project, not simply preparation for the visit. Inevitably, this meeting established a relationship between me and the visitor which influenced the subsequent situation.

Where a visitor believed in the meeting with the young people, that his relationship with me needed to be preserved, at the expense of his relationship with the group, then it was clear that the preparation meetings had been a failure because all I had done was to capture the visitor and failed to give him freedom to work with the members of the group. It was also the case, that where a visitor tried to preserve his relationship with me, he prevented the group exploring his relationship with the body which he had been invited to come and represent. In other words, he was acting in a way which showed that he was either uncertain about that relationship and had to protect it or that he was hostile to young people and needed to avoid truly encountering them. It was certainly the case that such behaviour, whatever the reason, was experienced by the young people as hostile since it prevented them in what they had come together to do and what they felt a visitor had agreed to by coming to the meeting. In order to help the work of a group it was necessary for me to find ways of facing this in the session and it was at such points that I needed to be fully aware of the danger of colluding with the splitting of good from bad. If my contributions were not clearly based on the reality of the situation, then I would simply be causing a visitor to become a 'bad object' to the group and becoming a good one myself. Young people could learn little about authority from this.

THE RESPONSES OF YOUNG PEOPLE TO DEFENSIVE BEHAVIOUR IN VISITORS

The most consistent response to these different kinds of defence was apathy on the part of the young people. Groups would frequently become sunk in silence, leaving a visitor to do all the talking and myself struggling to understand and find a way through the problem. Any anger which might have been around on account of the failure of the visitor (and inevitably myself) became deeply suppressed and could only be expressed by attacking a neighbour in a desultory fashion, scuffing one's feet on the floor, turning one's back on the group or in the end staying away from subsequent meetings. The overt expression of this anger became almost impossible. Sometimes, where a visitor captured a group, as the magistrate did with his talk of being a father, they would cheer up for that session, but in the next, despair would increase and the anger be even more deeply buried than before. There would be no sense of hope.

It was very seldom that any group got openly angry with a visitor. Much rather, they denied their capacities for feeling anger, or for thinking, or any sense of having authority themselves to deal constructively with such behaviour on the part of a visitor. Yet it was clear that they silently blamed the visitor and myself for letting them down and leaving them feeling trapped.

What seems to me to be significant was that, though some visitors consciously admitted fear of being attacked directly by a group, what they really seemed to fear most was being ignored and fled from; yet this was the very behaviour they succeeded in producing in the young people. This seemed to be something they were unable to deal with in themselves, which they projected onto the young people, and were again unable to deal with.

6. Factors Influencing a Visitor's Behaviour in Relation to Young People

It would seem to be reasonable to suppose that a significant factor in a visitor's behaviour when meeting a group would be his own attitudes and feelings about young people in general. If he believed most young people to be wasters, delinquents, or addicted to drugs, then he might be expected to view these particular young people in that light and behave towards them accordingly when he met them. To some extent this was the case. It was also the case that, when young people were treated as if they were such kinds of person, there was a strong possibility that they would respond in a way confirming such expectations. But it did not emerge that a visitor's expectations about this were necessarily the most important factor.

A football manager was a visitor to a group of van boys, all regular attenders at the Arsenal football ground and occupiers of the notorious North Bank terrace. The manager's view of young football fans and their ilk was that they were hooligans, extremely dangerous and probably mentally deranged. He spent some time talking to me of his feelings about the case of the young clerk who was beaten with sticks by a group of boys, and left dying outside the gates of Putney Cemetery in the autumn of 1969. It was obvious that his picture of such young men was an extremely frightening one. In the actual meeting with the van boys, the discussion ranged over many things to do with football. Had he any regrets at no longer playing, particularly since he had been a distinguished amateur international himself? What did he feel about rough play in his team? How important was it for his team to win and how far did he feel anything was justifiable in order to win? What about the behaviour of spectators? For an hour-and-a-half the discussion was vigorous and the business of being a manager was explored and tested relentlessly. The young men had some knowledge of the business themselves and made good use of it during the session. In talking about the visit a few days later, the manager told me how impressed he had been by the courtesy and the intelligence of the group. He was especially complimentary about their intelligence. He had thoroughly enjoyed the meeting and would very much like a chance to visit another group. I asked him how he felt about them in relation to the kind of young people he had talked about before. 'They were quite different', he said - 'nothing like those others at all'. He talked in glowing terms for a few moments, so I asked him how he would have felt if he had been walking in the street near Highbury after a football match and had met that group of about a dozen boys coming towards him.

He paused for a moment and I could see him constructing a mental picture. A group of such 16 or 17-year-olds, in boots, jeans held up with braces and many of them with closely cut hair, walking shoulder-to-shoulder towards him, almost as they had sat round him in the meeting. He suddenly went quite white as he realised what he had done and how his mental image of young people in general was so divorced from the reality of this particular experience.

This example illustrates the way in which other factors had been operating in his meeting with the young men which had caused him to discard his fantasy about young people (at least temporarily) and had enabled him to deal more realistically with the actual persons he met. This was the fact that he felt that he had authority in that meeting and was also clear about the relationship between himself and the football club of which he was manager; he had a clear understanding of this, particularly the relationship between himself in his own role and other people taking roles within the club. That is to say, the structure of the club was real to him and something to which he was able to respond and have feelings, and from which he also drew some sense of support. All of which he could talk about with the group.

It was evident from my discussions with him about his job, before he visited the group, that the structure itself was one which was reasonably coherent. For him the nature of the authority of different people was on the whole clear; it was obvious who was responsible to whom and what each person was expected to achieve. There were areas in which there was some uncertainty, such as in the relationship between the Supporters' Club and the manager. In areas such as this, there were sources of disagreement and conflict, though in that instance in the end the manager was likely to be largely unaffected by the views of the Supporters' Club so long as the team's results were satisfactory.

What this adds up to, therefore, is that, as the van boys met this football manager, in a very real sense they met not only him but also the club for which he worked. They perceived and explored things which were part of him, but also more than him. To some extent this was seen to be the case because they followed the fortunes of his club for some weeks afterwards. The effect of working within a structure which was coherent, being clear about what one was being asked to achieve and able to recognise those to whom one was responsible for achieving it, was a recurrent feature with those who were able to respond constructively to the group situation.

One feature which occurred frequently with such persons was the fact that they had to account for themselves regularly to those in authority over them, to senior officers, boards of directors or similar people. Another was their frequent reference to having learned their job in the early stages by watching and modelling themselves upon more experienced colleagues. Some of them were also aware of how they were themselves now being used in the same way by their own younger colleagues and subordinates. What these people had in common was a sense of authority which they communicated to the young people they met, and to which the young people in their turn responded without any sense of defensiveness.

In the preliminary interviews I had, it was usually possible to assess a visitor's understanding of his own authority, both from what he said and from how he behaved in relation to me. Not everyone who visited a group had a very clear understanding of his or her authority. Nor were a number of people likely to have such a sense, given the structure of the bodies for which they worked. In exploring the structures from which such visitors as probation officers, child care officers, teachers and youth employment officers came, I frequently found myself at a loss to understand what they were describing. Discussion almost inevitably slipped round to the relationship between social worker and client or teacher and pupil, to the exclusion of any other relationships in which such adults might be involved, including both colleagues and superiors. What was usually evident was an individual working at doing a job, the nature of which he found it hard to articulate clearly without using phrases such as 'good relationships' or 'happiness'. These were frequently not able to be explored any further. More than this, it was the case that those working in such situations were very uncertain about whom they were responsible to for carrying out their different tasks. In testing what I understood about the structure which such people came from, I found that what I described was often different from the structures perceived by others who also worked in it.

Rather than feeling that I was meeting a person with authority in such instances, I felt I was meeting an individual split off from others. Many of them were pleasant and attractive people, often with ideals which were important to them, yet in discussing their jobs with them there was a sense that these ideals proved hard to express in practice. Added to this was a sense that the person felt that the blame for not being able to practise these ideals largely lay with 'the system' or at least with others within the system, yet because the structure was unclear it was not certain who could actually be held responsible for what.

The impression which was thus created was that the relationship between worker and client or teacher and pupil was the crucial relationship and that everything of importance was vested in this. This had the consequence of needing to try and exclude from it anything unpleasant or threatening, which

66

might be felt to harm the relationship.

Where I found such feelings and attitudes in a visitor before he came to the group, my prediction was that he would not be able to give the members of a group real freedom to explore either their own experience or the visitor's own professional beliefs, and my expectation was that such a visitor would use some device or other to defend himself. It might be by presenting himself in some other role, as did the magistrate described earlier, by behaving as if he had come to get information from the young people, or in some cases by virtually giving up. Whatever the device used it was probable that the task of the group would not in fact be carried out in that session. As has already been said this had extensive effects on the behaviour of the young people even if they were not immediately apparent.

It is important to note that no visitor in this kind of situation (with the possible exception of one probation officer) was able to say in the group that he worked in a confused and confusing job, that such and such was how he felt about it, and talk about how he coped with his feelings. That is to say, people in such roles were not able to let their own real experience in their role be explored by the young people they met; more often they hid that experience.

One factor in the group which was significant to the visitors was my own presence. It was apparent for many of them that my having met them before coming, and being in the group during the session, was an important influence on their behaviour. This therefore needs examination.

MY OWN RELATIONSHIP WITH VISITORS AND HOW IT WAS USED

Each of the groups I have taken have moved through a sequence of: meeting me alone; then meeting with myself and a visitor present; and then back to meeting with me alone. Because I have been the constant factor throughout the life of the group, there has been an inevitable need for young people to feel that there was something good in me and what I represented so that they could keep on coming back to the meetings. In the first sessions one of the issues which it was necessary to work through concerned seeing that, on one hand I represented hope and the possibility of a relationship which contained positive feelings, yet the experiences which I was concerned to explore aroused anxiety in young people and sometimes caused them anger and pain. It was significant that in the first two sessions of a series, when young people were talking about the situations they had experienced, the discussion frequently concerned the difficulty of both loving and hating the same person. One way in which groups attempted to cope with the problem in relation to me was to try to convince me that teachers, parents, employers, probation officers or child care officers were callous, malicious, unpredictable and so on; whereas their own behaviour towards me as they spoke, indicated that they felt (for the time being anyway) that I was obviously benevolent and cared about their welfare.

It was vital to the long-term development of the group that I should work through this unrealistic splitting of good from bad. If it were not tackled sufficiently in relation to me alone, the arrival of a visitor presented a group with a perfect opportunity to continue to put all their good feelings onto one adult and all their bad feelings onto the other. The likelihood was that they would invest me with the good ones and the visitor with the bad. Groups tried to take this opportunity on many occasions. This splitting, particularly the projection of their negative feelings onto a visitor, contributed to the stress which visitors had to cope with. Only occasionally did the young people put the negativity onto me. The reason for this was their need to preserve me if the whole series of meetings were to produce anything of value to them. An important opportunity for their learning about adult behaviour stemmed from recognising what was happening on such occasions. The capacity of each of us adults to grapple with these projections, both positive and negative, and to refuse to collude with an unreal view of ourselves, was open for examination by the young people at all times.

As has been said, during the last year I spent an increasing amount of time with visitors before and after they came to the group. The main reason for this was to identify factors which supported a visitor as he came to a group and used the preliminary interviews as an opportunity to do this. But another reason was that, as I increasingly recognised the complexity of the situation into which visitors were being introduced, it was clearly necessary to spend more time in preparation with them. In the first year of the Project twenty minutes to half-an-hour seemed to suffice, or even an extended telephone call in some cases; in this last year I met visitors to the groups for periods of up to four hours before they came. This time was usually split up into two or more sessions. I also met them afterwards for periods of upwards of two hours. This had a marked effect on how visitors behaved in a group. Most importantly, they became more aware of the necessity to consider what the group was about and what they might expect to happen. They were less inclined to make assumptions which were likely to prove unhelpful, and they were also better able to use their relationship with me. This enabled some of them to disagree with me during a session and eased my own feelings of wanting to protect a visitor when the going was hard. We were both more aware of each other as real people, which meant that it was more likely that our real personalities could be more involved during the session and so be more clearly evident to the members of the groups concerned; thus the adult parts of each of us were more likely to be available to the young people so that they could learn from them.

But even the time spent with visitors before the meeting had its problems. One was that I was often seen as an 'expert' on young people, usually at the expense of the visitor's own knowledge of how to behave with young adults.

A corollary of this was that some people came to feel that this particular kind of group was more complicated than 'ordinary' group meetings. They came to believe that there was some magic which was part of this group to which I was privy and they were not, so they must copy me closely or follow my remarks implicitly for the magic to work. It was noticeable that visitors who felt this way often put whole chunks of things they had discussed with me before the session into their remarks to the young people, whether they had been asked about these matters or not. There was also a marked tendency to keep looking at me as if to check my reactions to what they had said, rather than checking the reactions of the young people themselves. It was apparent that such visitors were attributing a greater authority to me than I really had, while at the same time denying their own authority arising from their own experience.

In order to work at this problem, it was important for me to try to keep in mind six sets of relationships:

(a) the visitor and the members of the group;
(b) the visitor and the institution from which he came;
(c) myself and the group;
(d) myself and the visitor;
(e) myself and the institution within which the group was meeting (and so implicitly the group members themselves with that institution);
(f) myself and the institution from which I came.

The first five of these were relationships to which I would draw most frequent attention publicly; the last was one which I needed to be aware of, but found it was not often useful to comment on except in the sessions when visitors were not present – these were the first two or three sessions and the review sessions at the end, especially when members of groups wanted to know why I was running the group.

The most consistent point to emerge from meeting visitors after a session was that they often found it hard to talk to me about an experience that I had shared with them. They almost invariably only wanted to hear from me what I thought of the meeting before they felt able to expose their own judgement about it. They found it hard to believe that I wanted to learn from them. Even when they did begin to talk they were trying to find out what they felt I wanted to hear, rather than seeing our meeting as an opportunity to explore the experience we had both shared in to try and learn from it. To some extent this was due to their own assumptions about my being involved in research: this meant that they expected me to have a series of questions to which I wanted answers, whereas what I was in fact interested in was their experience, in whatever way they wanted to talk about it. What questions I had were tools for exploration, not seeking easy answers. The problem was also partly due to the difficulty of a visitor feeling that my own assessment of the situation was likely to be more 'accurate' than his, even though his view of it was necessarily different from mine.

There were very few visitors able to say much of how they felt about my own role and behaviour in the session. They almost always said they felt I had been helpful, seldom being very specific about what it was that had been helpful. One unusually articulate visitor described the session as rather like being 'with a group of kids exploring a haunted house, frightened but compelled to go on'; and said that he had seen my role as being to 'contain the chaos' while he got on with the group. Others indicated in more mundane ways that my presence had held some promise of order and stability for them; few went on to say directly how far the promise was fulfilled. A number indicated that it was not, by remarking on the discomfort of the surroundings or the chairs or the awkward time of the meeting. Others made some criticism of the way in which I had prepared them for the meeting, feeling I had not told them some of the things they would have liked to know. But on the whole visitors gave me the feeling that I was above criticism, that as an 'expert' on work with adolescents, I really knew what was going on and my meeting with them was more of a kindness on my part than a genuine attempt to understand things further. What was lost when people felt this way about me was the fact that many of them had at least as much if not more experience of work with young people than I had, often in quite different settings from my own; a number of them had adolescent and grown-up offspring; all of them had had their own experience of growing up and finding their own place in the world. In other words, it was common for adults to lose their sense of authority as adults when they met me in preparation for coming to a group and in reviewing their visit.

The effect which I had on so many visitors was obviously very important to what happened in the sessions, as well as probably being important for other reasons. A possible interpretation is that I had not avoided colluding with the 'good' projections of a group and behaved in a way which ensured that if there were going to be difficulties in a session, the visitor would be the one who suffered most. Yet I do not believe that this is wholly accurate, because my frequent practice was to return when possible to visitors who had a difficult time and invite them again. In only one instance did someone refuse to help me a second time, and in his case I believe that he acted appropriately since he was no longer an active practitioner and should not therefore have come in the first place. If they had a sense of my having made it difficult for them they would have been unlikely to accept the second invitation, since I was the constant factor, the request coming from a different group of young people.

My own understanding of the reason for this behaviour is that it was the high degree of anxiety about young people amongst adults in general which caused these adults to feel inadequate at the prospect of meeting a group.

70

This sense of inadequacy caused them to need some point of reference which was felt to be secure; in this instance they chose to use me for this purpose. They tried to attribute to me special knowledge and insight to which they felt they could not have access. My problem was to be realistic with them about what I did know and what I did not know, believing that if they could perceive me with some degree of reality then visitors would be more realistic about themselves. Though I was often at least partially successful in this, where a visitor in a session continued to attribute unreal power to me as he de-skilled himself, what he actually did was to make a major contribution towards reducing the effectiveness of what power I really did have. The result was to make work in the session harder for everyone.

Because visitors were asked in to help young people learn about the nature and use of authority, including understanding about one's authority as an adult, when a person behaved in such a fashion in relation to me, he was unlikely to be much of a resource to the young people he met.

It is probable that such behaviour as this is common amongst many adults in society who feel that the business of helping young people grow up is the exclusive province of teachers, youth leaders and similar specialists. In so doing they devalue the significance of their own contribution to the process, and (in so far as the 'specialists' collude with the devaluation) also contribute to the weakening of what such people as teachers and youth leaders really can achieve.

7. Interpretations

THE NATURE OF AUTHORITY

The first of the four working hypotheses which have underlain all the work done in this Project has been that the problem of the use of authority is the central problem of young people between the ages of 14 and 21. It is now possible to offer a definition of how I have come to understand the notion of authority as a result of this experience. To some extent it is similar to what is sometimes called the 'functional' definition of authority. This is not to pretend that other people necessarily use the word in this way, but that if it is used thus in planning and exploring work with young people then certain kinds of things will be taken into account and certain outcomes are likely to arise. [1]

During the last three years I have become aware that authority is an element inherent in any situation in which groups of people come together. Because all groups exist to do something, certain members are given authority consciously and unconsciously to act in a way which contributes towards carrying out that task; that is to say, roles are allocated amongst members of a group, and a structure evolved through which group members can work together to achieve something upon which they are agreed. Where the group's task has been articulated and understood so that the roles and the activities through which the task is carried out are recognised and the boundaries appropriately defined, then each member of the group can be aware of both his own authority and the authority of others including his superiors, his colleagues and his subordinates. As a result of this recognition of people's roles in a situation and an understanding of each person's authority, then members of groups can experience freedom in relation to each other in carrying out their task.

But it is evident from most people's experience that even where groups feel that they know what their task is, the above description of a group's working does not appear to apply universally. In exploring this, W R Bion[2], the psychoanalyst, puts forward the hypothesis that every group operates at two levels simultaneously. At one level much of their behaviour can be interpreted as carrying out the task for which the group is met together; roles are allocated, boundaries are drawn, activities defined, statements made and decisions taken so that work is carried out, change and development take place. This level of behaviour Bion calls Work Level (W).

But not all a group's behaviour can be interpreted at this level; at times work is impeded, interfered with, diverted and sometimes supported by emotional forces which indicate that group members have made a tacit assumption which powerfully influences their behaviour, namely, that their basic purpose is to survive. Different ways are found to deal with stress, anxiety, uncertainty and other feelings which are believed to be threatening to the group's continuation as it is. This level of activity Bion calls the Basic Assumption Level (Ba). He identifies three particular ways in which this level presents itself: dependence, where the group behave as if they were met to receive sustenance, both physical and emotional, from one person; pairing, where the group are met to reproduce themselves; and fight/flight, where the group must attack or flee from something or somebody felt to threaten it. Subsequent work with small groups broadly supports Bion's hypothesis, though many students of small group behaviour would now suggest that dependence and pairing are related in much the same way as fight/flight. Other basic assumptions have been suggested, but are not generally agreed at the moment. In the examples given in Chapter 2, the probation officer mobilised Basic Assumption fight/flight and the headmaster mobilised Basic Assumption dependence.

Authority, in the sense I have come to understand it, is concerned with Work Level activity. Where tasks are made clear and roles are defined, then persons are able to use the authority they have by right of their role in the group to enable the task for which the group met to be carried out, to mobilise the emotions associated with the Basic Assumptions which support that task, and to control those which impede it. In particular, people are able to identify the boundaries relevant to the task and know who has authority to control these boundaries.

Authority, therefore, is given to people to further a task. When members of a group draw attention to that task, and the roles and boundaries through which it is intended that the task be carried out, then they speak with authority in the group. The continual struggle for the members of any group is to contribute at the Work Level of the group's activity and to control the intrusion of Basic Assumption activities which impede the task. It is the task of leadership to give the model of how this can be done. It is clearly evident that this conception of authority applies not only to single groups but to groups which form different units within a larger enterprise or institution. This means that in such situations people's authority does not simply derive from the group of which they are current members, but also from others which have a bearing on that group as it meets.

Though, as a human being, I am a member of many different groups, in the small working groups used in this Project I received authority from a number of specific groups which included the following:

Those responsible for the young people who become members of the groups, such as teachers, employers, probation or child care officers.

The Grubb Institute.

The members of the group themselves, who consented to meet me.

The visitors.

I have this authority in my role as leader to the extent that the group members and the relevant external groups to which I belong accept the task which I embody as the task of the group. Where this has not been accepted, the continuation of a group has always been in question. In fact the failure of the group from the Children's Department was the result of a lack of understanding on this point, both on my own and the child care officers' parts. I failed to understand the task of the Department in relation to its adolescent clients who were living at home and thus did not recognise the nature of the child care officers' authority; nor did the CCO's succeed in understanding the task of the group and the nature of my authority. Because of this a number of significant factors, which all affected the life of the group, particularly the authority of the parents and substitute parents, were not taken into account in the preliminary planning; it was not surprising that the group had to be stopped earlier than planned.

The members of the groups themselves have authority in the situation by virtue of their attendance and, where it occurred, through common membership of the institution from which the group is drawn. Where they recognise and accept the task of that institution, they are likely to have some understanding of their authority in it, as was shown by the change of behaviour on the part of the printers when they realised that the group was a recognisable part of the work of their firm.

The visitors to the groups have had authority by virtue of representing the body from which they come. In many cases this has been given formally because they were sent to the group following my approach to the head of the institution or part-institution to which they belonged, such as the Governor of the prison, the Commander of the police division, or the Chief Executive of the local authority. But others have not been given authority to attend in such a formal way, since they did not belong to such an institution. I had to approach magistrates, most of the priests, local teachers and borough councillors direct. It was evident that there was a slight difference between the behaviour of people who were sent by their institutions, and those whom I approached direct; the former tended to be able to offer a clearer

74

understanding of their authority in society, whereas the latter tended to behave more as if they were trying to do something for me than trying to represent something for someone else in the community. This was evident because the latter group were more likely to want me to tell them what I thought of the session when it was over, than were the former. I had the sense of them asking me to compliment them. It seemed that they were uncertain of the source of their own authority in this situation, tending to be over conscious of what authority they felt I had given them when I invited them to come. This meant that they were also likely to perceive inaccurately the authority of the rest of the group. It was significant that the group of young printers noticed this in the behaviour of some of their visitors and commented on it at the end of the series; others may have noticed it but did not comment.

But the boundaries between groups and within and between enterprises are not the only relevant boundaries in a situation. There is also the boundary of each person's own ego, that which distinguishes between what is inside and what is outside him, and the boundaries within each person which distinguish between the different parts of his own inner world, between his internal objects and part-objects. Thus, in addition to membership of the relevant groups of which one is a part in the 'here and now', receiving authority from them to work on their behalf in a situation, so also each person has authority by virtue of being in control of himself, from his capacity to relate what he does both to what is real inside him and to what is real outside him. That is to say, he has authority and responsibility for the way he uses himself, his knowledge and experience in whatever situation he finds himself.

But simply to have authority does not of itself mean that it is used appropriately. It seems in the experience of this Project, that the following factors contributed towards its proper use. Various incidents and examples have been given which illustrate the points about freedom and authority, and brief reference is made to them again:

i.   Since authority is given to roles which are created for the furtherance of a task, authority is recognised by others to the extent that the task is carried out. This accounted for the young printers' recognising my authority in relation to their firm because they understood the firm's task and could therefore recognise my authority.

ii. Since authority is given to control transactions across boundaries, within and between groups, the task system boundaries need to be drawn in appropriate places. If they are not located adequately, people will draw them in different places with resulting confusion about what is inside and what is outside. Visitors who were clear about the structure from which they came, behaved with more confidence than those who were unclear. Because the boundaries of the group taken for the Children's Department were not fully understood by anyone involved, this led to confusion which resulted in the failure of that group.

iii. The person who takes a role needs to be able to keep in touch with reality, or else his decisions about transactions across boundaries will become inconsistent and the task impeded. In the example of the visit of the probation officer which resulted in the boys leaving the room, I had lost touch with how the boys were feeling about the visitor; their feelings were an important part of the reality of the total situation. I became inconsistent in the way I behaved and the boys finally left.

iv. The person who takes a role involving the exercise of authority needs to be able to 'fill' that role; he needs to bring to it the skills, resources, attitudes and beliefs which are needed if he is to use appropriately the authority he is given. Where he does not 'fill' the role he will not be able to exercise the authority appropriately. The different probation officers described in this report clearly illustrate instances of both filling and failing to fill a role.

v. The person needs to know to whom he is accountable for how he uses the authority he has; in other words he needs to be able to perceive the boundaries of the systems, groups and individuals concerned and to know what he is doing to them through his actions. It was evident that visitors whose work was supervised, as in the work of policemen, or who had a single 'boss', were more at ease than those who felt they had no identifiable boss such as teachers or careers advisory officers.

An important consideration linked with the use of authority was that those over whom it was exercised appropriately, experienced freedom as they took their own roles in the group, which also contributed to task performance. Those emotions, which were irrelevant to the task in which they were engaged, were able to be contained without a sense of deprivation or denial. They were thus able to use their own resources and skills and it was likely that not only was task performance achieved with a sense of satisfaction, but individuals experienced something of their own personal development as a result. This was evident not only in the groups but also at the EWR and Lyndhurst Clubs, where all the preceding points about authority were also observable.

Conversely, where these factors were not recognised by those using authority, their actions were experienced by others as hostile and punitive. In those cases where a person behaved in a way which cut across boundaries of which people were aware, they acted in an authoritarian manner. More difficult to cope with were those who used a charismatic approach (as did the headmaster with the further education students), the effect of which was to cause young people to forget different boundaries, allowing them to be obliterated. In so doing they effectively handed over their own authority to the charismatic leader and regressed into immature behaviour. Because those who followed such leadership were often not aware of what was being done to them until too late, they were then left in a situation which they could no longer influence or change, no matter how much they wished. When they emerged from the spell they found themselves bereft and felt they had been betrayed. This was evident in other groups and has been described in earlier passages of this report.

ADULTHOOD

As this Project has progressed it has become apparent that what it means to be an adult is something obscure in our present society. Some time ago it was fashionable to talk of 'maturity' but that is now an expression which seems to be out of vogue and has not been replaced. It still seems to me to be a meaningful term and is useful in this Project. The term 'adult' is frequently used as an adjective to describe films, plays and books, indicating that they are about either sex or violence in a way which was not common some ten years ago. Nevertheless, underlying all the work with young people in schools, colleges, universities and clubs, is an assumption that the purpose of the work is to help them become responsible adults in their turn. To put the same thing another way − to help young people develop towards their full stature. This assumption is largely taken for granted and is therefore often overlooked, particularly in moments of stress. Looking back on the behaviour of those who have visited different groups of young people over the last three years, it seems possible to make some attempt at a definition of adulthood which is workable in examining examples of behaviour, to help decide whether or not they could be called 'adult'. As elsewhere in this report what is intended is to describe activities and behaviour, not to classify individuals, though that may well be a consequence of such a description. It is important, however, to point out that no individual maintains a constant sophistication in his behaviour, but that at different times and in response to different circumstances he may act more or less maturely. How he acts could therefore conceivably be plotted as points on a continuum between 'maturity' and 'immaturity'.

Where the behaviour of visitors has seemed mature, that is to say, it has called forth constructive responses from the young people present, or at least made it possible for such responses to emerge, the following factors have appeared to exist together in such behaviour:

i.   The recognition of what is real in oneself and one's own experience, in other words to have a sense of one's own identity.

ii. The recognition of what is real in others and in their experience, or to recognise their identity.

iii. The capacity to recognise what is the appropriate relationship to be established between persons who are together in a specific situation, thus enabling the recognition and distinction of what is relevant and real from what is real but may be irrelevant at that particular moment. The appropriateness will depend on the extent to which the task for which people are met together is carried out through those relationships.

To isolate these factors in this way is not to say anything which is of itself new. There are definitions of sanity which refer to the same three, for example David Wood writing in 'New Society' about the work of R D Laing. 'Sanity consists in a sense of ourselves existing firmly in the world, thereby being able to experience others as existing in the same way and having reciprocal relations with them.' [3]

The same points are made in a different way by Erik Erikson in a passage in his book 'Identity' in which he describes the problem of adulthood as 'to **take care** of those to whom one finds oneself committed as one emerges from the identity period, and to whom one owes **their** identity' (Erikson's stressing). What Erikson draws out clearly in this passage is the responsibility of the adult to be depended upon by others who need to be able to use his experience. His definition puts the three factors of adult behaviour together in a specific context though in slightly different terms.

To interpret this in relationship terms: no one develops an understanding of their own identity alone, but as a result of interaction with others. It is from the way each person sees himself reflected back to him that he can know what he is. Further than this, identity is not necessarily fixed, but has a potential to grow and develop as people enter different situations and incorpora' different experiences and models into themselves. Part of an adult's identity arises from his being a member of the sentient group of adults with all its infinite variety of other sub-groupings, both task groupings and sentient groupings. As members of the sentient group of adults, what we all have in common is that we are all growing older and approaching death, the final boundary of the group. We are helped to identify what it means to be an adult by observing how others cope with this process by interacting with them and by being aware of how we are coping with its problems ourselves. Clearly, given the vastness of the size of the whole sentient group of adults and the general length of time of the whole process of growing old, it is difficult for each individual to comprehend what is entailed if he only contemplates it at this level. It is through being aware of the process on a smaller scale, in groups of a size we can comprehend, in spans of time which we can take account of, that we can develop our awareness of the whole. Thus again our adulthood is perceived, both by us and by others, through structures which are recognisable and tasks which can be identified. If we are not able to perceive our own adulthood in this way, then it is likely that we will either

abandon it or try to find other ways of making it apparent; most likely by
contrasting ourselves with those who are not yet adult. But if we do this, as
the work of the Project indicates we are doing, then we distort our perception
of both what we are and what they are. We will not give true value to ourselves
nor to them: as a consequence, adulthood will be perceived by those who
approach it as undesirable since we have failed to discover what is desirable
in it for ourselves.

Time, and a sense of the impact upon the present of the past, is a further
significant factor in adult behaviour. At one level this links up with the
questions of having a belief in the validity of one's own experiences as a
human being: part of adult authority stems from this fact of experience. In
another way, to have this sense of time also enables a realistic view of the
nature of development to be held; without a sense of time the notion of development becomes nonsensical. But part of the problem of having an awareness
of the past is that it can become a trap from which one cannot escape; part of
the challenge of adult behaviour is to be prepared to test the past continually
and thus discover its relevance to the present and the future. This requires
a capacity to recognise mistakes and failures, to seek to overcome their
consequences, as well as the capacity to recognise when one has been right
and to be prepared to stand by that. Unless time and the past are viewed in
these terms, once again development and growth become nonsensical; the
excessive preservation of history produces stagnation, not growth. Thus
adult behaviour depends upon a sense of a process going on; a process which
is evident in time. Awareness of the dimension of time enables the nature of
the process to be raised to consciousness in its turn. The process can then
be supported, diverted or even halted in a way which enables us to know what
we are doing and, possibly, why.

The significance of understanding both time and process are stressed by
two recent Canadian writers, Professors Houghton and Northrop Frye.
Professor Houghton suggests that one of the consequences of failing to see a
continuous process is the emergence of the myth of intergenerational conflict
as an alleged underlying principle of human behaviour. He rejects intergenerational conflict as a principle but sees it rather as observable phenomenon
which needs to be interpreted in relation to the process itself. He makes the
point that we are now reaching a crisis for all of us as a result of the failure
to take account of the process. [5]

Professor Northrop Frye points to the danger of contrasting the 'long
view' with the 'immediate view', as happens in much of present day radicalism.
He goes on:

"A less attractive side of the same situation (taking the immediate view)
is the general panic, even hysteria, that the loss of reference to temporal
context has left us with. The most obvious form of this panic is the
flight from the past: the anxiety to be up-to-date, to be rid of unfashionable

ideas and techniques, to condemn everything unsatisfactory with the same formula, that it is too cumbersome and obsolete for the unimpeded movement assumed to be necessary today."

What is striking about his essay is his belief that the crisis with which we are presented as a result of this, is a religious one, 'that contemporary radicalism is deeply, even desperately, religious both in its anxieties and in its assertions'. (6)

In talking with members of groups about how they perceived adulthood, two points emerged again and again. On one hand they desired the 'freedom' of being an adult, 'being able to go where I like and do what I like'; on the other hand they feared 'the responsibilities of having a family and children'. It would not have been surprising to find these attitudes amongst people aged 12 or 13 but they were common amongst those of 17, 18 or 19. It was apparent from this that their perception of what it means to be an adult, even when on the threshold of adulthood themselves, is crude and undeveloped. Inevitably this reflects on the model of adulthood presented to them by those they see as being adults.

Because it is through the structures to which people belong that it is possible to begin to be aware of what it means to be an adult, we are brought back again to the notion of authority. The three factors present in adult behaviour concern the recognition and control of boundaries in relation to task, the boundaries being both personal and institutional ones, hence the relevance of authority.

From this it is possible to draw together these interpretations of authority and the nature of adulthood in the context of the experience of this Project, remembering that it has worked largely with those aged between 15 and 17. It is worth recognising that what happens to people of this age is likely to influence how they develop and what kinds of 19, 20 and 21-year-olds they become.

It has been apparent and commented upon, that the adults who have been able to establish the most constructive relationships with the young people they have met, have been those who were aware of their authority both as adults and in the role they take in society. It has been those who have been able to show by their behaviour what it means to be an **adult** policeman or an **adult probation officer,** who have been experienced by the young people as a resource and to whom they have been able to respond constructively. Where visitors have been uncertain of their authority in these terms, their behaviour has been defensive and was experienced by those they met as hostile and punitive, no matter what was the intention of the visitor. The doctor who simply behaved as a doctor, and did not allow them to perceive how an adult feels in his role as a doctor, was experienced as hostile by the young people because he caused them to feel like patients – which they were not. The referee who told stories about his earlier life was similarly experienced because he made the boys feel like children; the probation officer who showed neither his authority as an adult nor as a probation officer was perceived as so punitive that the boys fled from him and immediately retaliated on the adult world when they got outside.

To be able to maintain one's role as an adult and a particular role in society has meant being prepared to accept the feelings of young people towards whatever it is one represented to them; these may be feelings of interest and affinity as a group of boys have had for a football manager; or they may be feelings of anger and hostility as they have had for a teacher or policeman. Or a person may simply be seen as an adult and stripped of his authority as anything else. For instance a young man on probation said of his probation officer aged about 45, 'He is a senile member of another generation and is irrelevant to me'. These feelings needed to be recognised, faced up to and worked through in order to reach some understanding of the reality of what each person represented. Until this was done no real development could take place.

As an adult in these groups I have had to work out how to use the real feelings towards me. At times young people have been exceedingly angry with me, often finding themselves unable to express it; at other times I have been angry with them yet not known how to use my anger. At times both I and groups have felt we were getting on famously with little real evidence about why. It has been important to find out what was the best way to further the task of a group and make use of such feelings whatever they were. In these instances I often found that my role as the leader of the group was at stake, with all that entailed, including the roles of other members of the group but more especially my own adulthood being tested to and sometimes beyond the limit. Where I was able to tolerate the stress involved, without defending myself for my own sake, then growth and development were a consequence, not only for the young people but also for me; where I failed, either by abdicating or behaving defensively, they were caught up in my failure, often without understanding that this had happened, beyond experiencing feelings of being frustrated and betrayed which they may not have been able to attribute consciously to me.

The supports which have particularly enabled me to work at this problem have arisen from my having a real sense of working on behalf of other groups of people whose task I understood. Where I was uncertain of this, then my behaviour when in contact with young people conveyed this uncertainty and they found it difficult to work with me. The clearest case of this arose in the failure of the Children's Department group. It has been on the basis of my own real interaction with other adults, my recognition of their tasks, roles and boundaries (including deadlines of time) that I have been helped to grapple with the problems of my own adulthood. I have then been able to help young people to grapple with theirs. I have already explored the same issue as it appeared to relate to other people in the group.

NOTES

(1) It is important to note that the conception of authority explored here is not an idiosyncratic one which would not be accepted by others working in other fields and with other disciplines. Though this is not the place to contrast the conception with other important ones it is worth pointing out that it accords with Professor H L A Hart's use of it in – The Report of the Committee on Relations with Junior Members – (OUP 1969), especially in paragraphs 23-39. This passage was described by Professor Bernard Crick, Professor of Politics at Sheffield University, as '... one of the best statements on the nature of legitimate authority I have ever read. It should be in the texts of political philosophy.'

Furthermore, what has been said here about authority also links with the way Elliot Studt uses it in her essay, 'Worker-client authority relationships in social work' in – New Developments in Casework – edited by Dame Eileen Younghusband (George Allen and Unwin 1966)

(2) W R Bion   Experiences in Groups   Tavistock Publications 1961

(3) D Wood   The Four Gospels   New Society 18 December 196

(4) E Erikson   Identity, Youth in Crisis   Faber and Faber 1968 p 33

(5) V P Houghton   The Myth of Intergenera-   University of Nottingham,
                     tional Conflict   Institute of Education
                                                  Education Papers No 11 1970

(6) Northrop Frye   The University and Personal Tavistock Publications 1969
                     Life – in W R Niblett ed. –
                     'Higher Education - Demand
                     and Response'

8. The Transition to Full Adulthood

In many earlier societies, and in some current ones, the transition to membership of the adult world has been clearly marked by different kinds of rites and initiation ceremonies. Up to the point of the ceremony, the young person can recognise that he is viewed as taking one kind of fundamental role, a role in which he is not likely to be expected to carry great responsibilities for anyone other than himself. (He may even be excused that sometimes.) He is expected to give precedence to those who are his elders (and possibly, in some cases, his betters). Following his initiation – a puberty rite – the young person is now viewed and expected to view himself in a different light. He is now an adult. Roger Barnard [1] points out the complexity of this change in that 'the purpose and effect of conducting people across those difficult thresholds of transformation ... demand a change in the patterns not only of conscious life but of unconscious life also'. The successful realising of the transformation is not of itself achieved by the ceremony; in fact the full transformation is probably never made by any individual because man always tends to regress and fall back on immature patterns of behaviour when under stress. What is certainly achieved is that the person who goes through the ceremony can now legitimately **feel** that he belongs to the sentient group of adults and has left the sentient group of children and young people behind. Now he is seen by others to have done this.

In all our present societies we have no clear marking of the boundary between adults and young people. In fact, the position is exceedingly unclear in a great many instances (even though the Representation of the People Act of 1969 goes a long way to clearing up some of the most confusing aspects and anomalies from a legal point of view). Thus young people are uncertain to which sentient group they feel they belong and to which they feel that they are believed to belong.

Goffman [2] in his essay, 'Role Distance', provides important concepts which help in this examination. In talking of role he uses the terms 'commitment', 'attachment' and 'embracement'. To be 'committed' to a role refers not to the feelings of the person about taking that role, but to the way a situation, including the expectations of others, commits one to that role. Goffman defines commitment as the 'impersonally enforced structural arrangements'. For example, a young policeman arriving at the scene of an accident is committed to take a certain role in that situation by his uniform and the way other people behave towards him. To be 'attached' means that the person feels emotionally attached to that role; he wishes to be seen in such a role and receives satisfaction from it. Goffman puts it that 'the self image available is one with which a person becomes effectively enamoured and sees himself in terms of enactment of the role and the self identification emerging from this enactment'. [3] The young policeman mentioned earlier may or may not be attached to his role in the situation, possibly depending on the nature of the accident and the extent to which he is able to cope with it. In talking of 'embracement' of a role, three matters are involved for the person: (i) an 'admitted or expressed attachment'; (ii) a demonstration of the qualifications and capacities for performing it; (iii) an 'active engagement or spontaneous involvement in the role activity at hand, that is, a visible investment of attention and muscular effort'. Goffman goes on: 'To embrace a role is to disappear completely into the virtual self available in the situation, to be seen fully in terms of the image, and to confirm expressively one's acceptance of it. To embrace a role is to be embraced by it'. [4]

To relate these concepts to the situation of young people. There are two major roles available to them if they are aged between 14 and 18, the role of 'adult' and the role of 'young person'. Because of their image and their inevitably ambivalent feelings about growing up, they are uncertain as to which role they are **attached**. At different times and by different people (often seemingly arbitrarily) they find that they are **committed** to either one role or the other. As a result of these uncertainties, they are likely to find it hard to begin to become **attached** to the role to which they know they will soon be

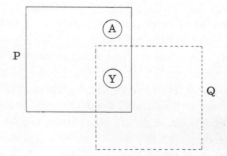

Figure 9. Two persons in a situation where their membership of the two groups, adults and young people, overlaps. If Y is taken as being a young person, the diagram indicates his uncertainty about how to behave in the situation where he is aware of both his membership of the adult group P and the group of young people Q. The most important resource to help him work out how to behave will be an adult A who can express his own embracement of the adult role through his behaviour

committed by the combination of their physiological development, their impending legal status and the expectations of others. This situation can be represented diagrammatically as in Figure 9. This diagram has been simplified to indicate an overlapping of only two groups, that of adults and young people; in practice there are likely to be many others which make the total situation more complex, especially for young people.

In Goffman's terms the successful end product of a series of such situations is a young person who embraces his adult role. Merton has called this process 'anticipatory socialisation'. [5] He goes on to describe it as:

> "The acquisition of values and orientations found in statuses and groups in which one is not yet engaged but which one is likely to enter ... much of such preparation is **implicit, unwitting** and **informal**, and it is particularly to this that the notion of anticipatory socialisation directs our attention."

The process by which one joins a sentient group is only partly, and probably least importantly, by the simple acquisition of skills and knowledge. More importantly the process is one of what J W M Whiting calls **identification**, [6] and Goffman would call embracement. This is a process by which one learns about the role one intends to take up through interaction with someone who takes that role, which results in modelling one's own behaviour on that of others, by introjecting parts of the other into one's own inner world. Initially it is likely that the interaction is between persons in two separate roles. The point being made is that the process of identification by which young people move to taking full adult roles is one initially of interaction in adult/young person roles and subsequently in adult/adult roles. It is through this process that it is possible to begin to understand what a young person is attaching himself to, while being able to maintain some distance from it because he is not yet fully committed. All this takes place in a special and often unrecognised way. To quote Merton again:

> "... anticipatory socialisation is not didactic. The individual responds to the cues in behavioural situations more or less unwittingly, draws implications from these for future role behaviour, and thus becomes orientated towards a status he does not yet occupy. Typically he does not expressly codify the values and role-requirements he is learning." (7)

Interestingly enough, this passage illustrates Figure 9 yet again. The significant point about the adult role is that in itself it is not overtly codified in the way many other roles are. Nevertheless it has a coherence which has already been endorsed here. There is an assumed adulthood which underlies the basis of the laws which are enforced and the demands which are made of those who are regarded as responsible citizens in a wide variety of different settings. What the young person is asked to do during these transitional stages of his life is to piece together his own understanding of the adult role, with his own modifications to fit the way he himself takes that role. By introjecting those parts of the adult role which he perceives in the adults whom he encounters, he builds up a conception of adulthood which becomes an object in his inner world affecting the way in which he behaves. Insofar as he builds up a good object, the young person begins to attach himself to the role of an adult. If he builds up a bad object, he will distance himself from it and reject it.

From this it is evident that the transition to adulthood will be facilitated by providing clear and coherent descriptions and models of what it means to be an adult. The effect of this is to help the young person to understand realistically what will be entailed by his own adulthood and he can take steps to prepare himself for it. What this especially demands of everyone concerned both adults and young people, is particular understanding of the **adult aspect** of the transition and for attention to be focused on that aspect. It is in these terms that the remark made earlier, about adults who have successfully made that transition being the most important resources to help others to do the same, should be understood.

The present behaviour of many young adults, such as students and other people of a similar age, indicates that what has been perceived is believed to be undesirable, to be rejected and ultimately overthrown. It is a comment on the nature of adulthood as it has been communicated to them. When they declare 'We are the writing on your wall', in seven words they spell out for us our failure as individuals to communicate to them that there are worthwhile things about being adult; our failure to take hold, in our own ways, of the problems which confront us all as human beings; our reluctance to grapple with the problem of being compromised by the society in which we live. They challenge each adult and they challenge the Establishment supported by us adults who have failed to use our skills, knowledge, experience and resources to make that Establishment represent something of which we can be proud rather than ashamed.

NOTES

(1) R Barnard   Initiation by Violence: The Uses   New Society 27 June 1968
                 of Delinquency

(2) E Goffman   Where the Action Is   Allen Lane
                                         Penguin Press 1969

(3)   Ibid p 43

(4)   Ibid p 60

(5) R K Merton   Social Theory and Social   The Free Press 1957
                 Structure   p 384 ff

(6) For further study on this see:

    J W M Whiting   Identification and Resource   University of Texas
                    Mediation - in Personality   Press 1960
                    Development in Children
                    Ed. I Iscoe and H Stevenson

(7) R K Merton   op. cit - p 385

9. The Predicament of the Young Adult

The Young Adult Resource Project began work in a climate of opinion which seemed to postulate that the crisis area for work with young adults lay in the provision of resources to help those from disadvantaged social backgrounds to overcome their linguistic, intellectual and social handicaps. Our own original hypotheses led us to believe that the real crux of the problem lay much deeper, in factors to do with authority and adulthood which were actually obscured by the social handicap question, important though that was. A result of concentration on that issue, especially by most sociologists, was the mis-interpretation of the significance of the work of such people as Frank Musgrove (1965), the Eppels (1966), David Downes (1966) and others, who in different ways pointed to the underlying problems of the relations between adults and young people in general. The policies of comprehensivisation of schools, raising the school leaving age, the growth of counselling services, the expansion of higher education, and the development of detached rather than club work by the youth service, have all gone ahead without examination in the light of these issues.

For over three years in working on this Project I was involved in the lives of young people, in formal and informal settings. I met them in schools, at work, at college, on probation, under the care of the Children's Department and in youth clubs; I mixed with them in the streets, cafes and pubs; I was involved with their families, both in good times and in bad. Some people I met only once or twice; I met nearly one hundred and fifty over periods lasting from three to six months; with a couple of dozen I was involved for the whole three-and-a-half years, seeing them leave school, grapple with the problems of beginning work, and had the fortune to see two or three get married and have their first child.

On the basis of relating observations of the experimental situation of the small working groups, the varied experiences of other kinds and the research work of other people, it is now possible for me to offer a description of the predicament of the young person leaving school and taking up different roles as a full member of adult society. In the first place the most important

consistent help to a young person at this stage is provided by opportunities
for interaction with adults who have themselves made the transition to adulthood successfully and who can maintain this in their dealings with young people
Interaction which is solely or largely limited to one's peer group is likely to
lead to regression into less mature patterns of behaviour, particularly to a
state of depression and sterility from which it will be difficult to break out.
Sometimes it leads to outbursts of anger and aggression which may easily
become wildly uncontrolled in specific situations such as large meetings,
demonstrations and in football crowds. Where young people become gathered
together in large numbers, the problem for any adult who becomes involved
with them is to resist the enormous inevitable pressures either to forsake his
own adulthood and his authority as an adult and become another 'young person'
in his behaviour or else to try and defend himself by abdication or irrational
behaviour. It seems to me from my experience that one adult can maintain a
reasonable level of interaction with up to ten or a dozen young people at any
one moment; where the ratio is higher than that, the pressures on his adulthood progressively build up and the quality of the interaction between himself
and the young people begins to deteriorate. In Goffman's terms he becomes
'committed' to an 'adolescent' rather than an 'adult' role. It thus becomes
less valuable to all involved.

What particularly emerges from herding young people together is the
development of symbols, stereotypes and myths on the part of both adults and
young people – stereotypes which may form the basis of behaviour, but which
actually obscure reality. A student can leap up on the platform and shout at
a Parliamentary Select Committee which is trying to understand the current
situation in universities, 'You are bloody irrelevant', and a University Vice-
Chancellor can refuse to deal with two students over the issue of political files
because they are not wearing ties. Each can feel that his action is justified
and well supported, yet each action obscures the real points and problems at
issue.

At the present moment the assumption underlying a great deal of work
with young people is that they want to be kept together, that they really want
the sole company of their peers. My own experience over the last three years
indicates that, although they may like the opportunity to be with people of their
own age, they are also deeply concerned, especially between the ages of 15
and 18, to have opportunities to be with adults and to interact realistically
with them.

One 15-year-old described his feelings about dealing with adults: 'It's
like building a bridge over a gap. We each push out towards each other; when
we meet in the middle, then we are really talking. When that happens, I get
a tremendous feeling of excitement down here in the pit of my stomach'. But
he went on, sadly: 'The trouble is that most adults start out higher than us,

so we never meet'. It is probable that the continual failure to meet has now had some serious effect on him and influences his present behaviour.

It is interesting to reflect that many adults may recognise the same description as part of their own experience. Lord Robertson, speaking in the Lords' debate on Youth and the Nation in 1968, said:

"... my own experience ... is that when I talk to them and our conversation comes to an end I find myself, as I say goodbye, most grateful to them for taking so much trouble and for being, apparently at all events, so interested in the few opinions I have offered them.' (1)

Yet so many of the situations which are provided, within which young people and adults come together, actually militate against the kind of interaction here described.

But simply to provide situations in which a reasonable proportion of adults and young people meet together is not of itself sufficient to make the interaction creative, as the experience of the small working groups has gone to show. It is also necessary for the adults involved to be able to retain and use their authority as adults. Much of the evidence of this Project shows how difficult this has been. Partly this is so because it is in itself a difficult thing to do. Professor Ben Morris, writing in the 'New Era', recognises this:

"We have practically everything to learn about understanding the stresses and conflicts of childhood in the sense of trying to help children to tolerate them and use them, not defensively to limit and shut out reality, but constructively to reveal reality through creation and discovery. If we have to learn how to do this with children, have we not first in fact to learn how to do it ... with ourselves? This is likely to be a promethian task.

"A great deal of the time we are apt to deny that there is any such task. Our defences against inner reality in particular are often so good that for long spells we exist by accepting complacently the deadening routine of our formal educational procedures."

He goes on:

"The rejection we mete out so much of the time to children and young people is a concealed way of rejecting something in ourselves that we do not wish to acknowledge, something based on fear or hate or envy." (2)

The problem of maintaining one's own adulthood is also made difficult for many because it is often not perceived as being of importance to young people. Numerous visitors to groups, some quoted in this report, have not recognised what their adulthood meant in the situation. But the same view is also held, at least by implication, by people of considerable influence on work with young people. In the, by now almost standard, text book on the sociology of education, 'Education, Economy and Society' (3), J Kob writes of the teacher's role:

"The teacher's specific professional functional sphere is the world of youth, organised in schools: his belonging to the adult world outside has nothing to do with his profession."

Where adults have failed to understand the nature of their authority, either as adults or in specific roles in society, their behaviour has been experienced by young people who meet them as hostile and punitive. This is not to say that the conscious motivation of the adult has always been hostile, but that their behaviour has been perceived as such by those towards whom it was directed, much as soft furry objects in John Steinbeck's 'Of Mice and Men' experienced the attentions of Lenny.

The hostility of adults has not, however, always been unconscious. In fact, the more certain stereotypes have emerged, resulting from lumping young people together, the more conscious the hostility becomes. Frank Musgrove demonstrates this statistically in 'Youth and the Social Order', but there are other examples of incidents which can be pointed to. 'The Guardian', on 12 July 1969, published an article headed, 'Mob-law week' about how 300 local inhabitants attacked 21 young beatniks in St Ives. Judith Cook, the writer, included a paragraph which read:

"By midnight the police, their backs to the wall, were repelling constant rushes of young men screaming 'String them up! ', egged on by a solid mass of people whooped up to fever pitch. The behaviour of the police under extreme provocation deserves nothing but praise."

The people whom the police were defending were the beatniks who had taken over a cottage in the town and were being attacked by the crowd of local residents. Or again, when students were lobbying for higher grants in March 1968, two points emerged. J P Mackintosh, MP, in an article in 'The Times Educational Supplement' [4] commented that his Labour colleagues were strongly opposed to the request for a 10s a week increase in student grants, yet the same MP's would have been likely to be strongly in favour of even higher demands from young people of the same age but at work. At the same time two MP's tabled a motion in the House of Commons which accepted as inevitable some modest increase in student grants, adding that they trusted that: 'Only a small proportion of this increase will be absorbed by the rising prices of knuckledusters, marbles, blackjacks and stink bombs, regarded in some student circles nowadays as apparently essential items of modern educational equipment. '

Current newspapers writing about 'skinheads' evidences the same hostile attitudes towards young people of a different background from the students.

But the hostilities can also be expressed towards individuals and for an example one can turn again to the Lord's debate on Youth and the Nation. Early in the debate Lord Faversham, aged 22, spoke describing what it feels like to be a young man today, and amongst a number of remarks from that point of view he said:

"As a young man I find myself to be public property and I must assume it is for the better." (5)

It was significant that, although numerous subsequent speakers referred to his speech, only one peer took what he said seriously. The others dismissed it in various rejecting and condescending remarks, such as 'Extravagant, much of it preposterous and all of it rather splendid' [6]; and 'Not typical in its cynicism'. [7]

But despite the hostility of adults towards them, young people are not individually hostile towards adults, but are more likely to recognise realistically their dependence upon them. The direct evidence of this Project is supported by Frank Musgrove [8] and Pearl Jephcott [9]; the latter found that young people in Glasgow were more sorry for adults than hostile towards them; they also bemoaned the lack of informal meeting places for themselves and adults. The way in which large numbers of young people present themselves to Task Force, the Young Volunteer Force Foundation, Community Service Volunteers and Shelter as paid and voluntary workers is often indicative of the large amount of goodwill which they have towards the adult world.

Bernard Davies points out:

"A great deal of education, not least in the youth service, still seems to be carried out on the assumption that it is only to greater affluence, independence and alienation among the young that adults must respond. Yet the first need is to help youth out of its strait-jacket.

In traditional youth organisations, youth clubs, the Duke of Edinburgh's Award, Young Volunteer Force and in schools themselves, the motives for exploiting what is socially 'beneficial' and damming up what is socially 'destructive' still predominates. Control remains the first, though rarely explicit, priority. Genuine teenage self-expression – which ... at present we have not got – is still an undervalued and even feared objective." (10)

So even the good will which young people have towards the adult world is exploited and turned against them.

It seems to be the case that adults do not at present want young people to grow out of this mess. David Downes points out:

"The concept of the teenage role is the product of external cultural forces, but the celerity with which it became rooted testifies to the immensely powerful 'generational' need it fulfilled." (11)

The 'cultural forces' he particularly cites include the commercial need for a market which was pointed to by Mark Abrams in his study on teenage consumer spending. [12] But other forces include the increased length of educational careers and the raising of the school leaving age which reinforce the young person's separation from adults.

E M Eppel, in his lecture 'The Adolescent Predicament', points to the danger:

"There are others who believe that the teenage culture provides a weak and unsatisfactory solution to the tasks of the adolescent. He may drain off unnecessary tensions into an encapsulated world characterised by a great deal of conformity and lack of individuality.

> ... When we ... reflect that we are soon to be faced with an extra year of compulsory education, we may see that the predicament may become even more acute unless teachers think very hard about the nature of the development of the adolescent as a whole and about how the enforced prolongation of dependent status may at least be mitigated by practices that help to build up the adolescent's self esteem and meet his legitimate needs to be accorded some kind of independent status." (13)

Even the wise recommendations of the Latey Committee on the 'Age of Majority' had to undergo powerful opposition, even a short period when it looked as though they would come to nothing, before finally being incorporated into the Representation of the People Act 1969. What we now face is the situation where, at one level, we encourage young people to take up adult roles at an earlier age, while, on the other hand, we encourage more and more to remain in a dependent state, **in statu pupillari**, for longer and longer. It is not surprising that this schizophrenic message is resulting in large numbers of third year undergraduates in the Lent term had not made up their minds what career they intended to follow after Summer 1970, or that student rebellions break out, providing another way of dealing with stress.

What is clear, is that at work young people are most able to cope with the confusion which is presented to them by the adult world. It is at work that processes become easily evident, that people can have a sense of participating in those processes, and derive a sense of purpose from them. It is worth noting that the behaviour of young employees at conferences run by such bodies as the Industrial Society, show that they usually support their boss, rather than the unions. This report has already commented on the more sophisticated behaviour of young employees, their greater capacity to cope with stress and anxiety and their greater tenacity than those in other, particularly educational, situations. It is in the setting of employment that conflict can be mobilised constructively, both by adults and young people, since ways of using it are more easily discerned; adults are more secure themselves and find young people less threatening than in other settings. Problems of authority are better able to be worked at and do not seem to be found overwhelming.

This is also confirmed by other people. Jeremy Bugler, in an article on 'skinheads', shows that they give great importance to their work. (14) The Home Office Research Unit's study, 'Probationers in their Social Environment' found that, of all the settings in which they studied the attitudes of those on probation, the place where leadership and authority were most likely to be seen as supportive was at work. (15) The author, Martin Davies, points out that 85.8% of probationers said they did not feel pushed around by their immediate bosses; only 9.4% felt there was no one with authority for whom they felt any warmth; and only 11.8% expressed real dislike for any of the authority figures at work. He goes on:

"The social network in his job environment may play a large part in his feeling of acceptance or rejection in the world at large."

The Schools Council Enquiry No 1 found that for 19 and 20-year-olds who had left school early, their career and work rated as of the greatest importance to them; this was also true of the 15-year-olds. The Eppels, studying 15 to 18-year-olds on day release, found that:

"There is a considerable amount of potential personal identification with work and a fairly strong feeling of personal responsibility to complete what has been undertaken." (16)

Peter Willmott, in his study of adolescent boys in East London, suggested that the interest in work and careers on the part of his subjects was such that youth clubs should be properly equipped to help with guidance in this field. (17) Perhaps the whole problem is best summed up by a French boy who was quoted in 'The Guardian' as saying:

"Leisure is not the principal aspect of our preoccupation. Organising our leisure is above all, a means for adults to ease their conscience. Our main worry is our professional future." (18)

It is at work that young people begin to feel that they are treated as adults and begin to be able to respond constructively to this; thus they can take up their full adult roles with some sense of confidence.

The problem for the young adult is aggravated by many of the present approaches to helping him as he takes up his place in adult society. The opportunities provided ostensibly to help him in fact often encourage both him and the adults that he meets to regress because of the assumptions made in planning. Much of traditional youth club work and more recent developments such as detached work, the provision of counselling services and a number of the social service schemes such as Task Force and YVF operate in the young person's leisure time. Some of the difficulties about choice which are presented have already been explored here, but further than this Dr Ralph Glasser, author of the book, 'Leisure – Penalty or Prize', has said:

"The romantics thought of leisure as a way of releasing man's natural personality, which was bowed down by work. The whole social reform movement of the last 150 years is based on that idea. The last thing they foresaw was that leisure could ever be a burden. But this promise of automatic release has not been fulfilled ...

"The main aim (of the user of leisure) is a search for a satisfactory identity.

"The longing to forget that this search has failed leads to the boom in tranquilisers and other oblivion makers. And this is why people chase after folk heroes – such as the Beatles and Elizabeth Taylor – who seem to have the certainty and the free will they themselves lack." (19)

All this points to how the approaches of adults can divert young people from those issues and situations in the exploration of which real development and growth take place. It is not surprising, therefore, that many young people increasingly take refuge in drugs and sexual activity, the consequences of both of which they clearly recognise to be potential disaster for themselves and for the rest of society; alternatively, they retreat into communal living situations where they drop out and re-enact the plight of exploited people such as American Indians. Yet even in writing that, one distorts the picture and fails to recognise, that, of the 18 to 24-year-old age group, over half are married and their main concern is the cost of living and the problem of getting a mortgage. [20]

The lesson of this Young Adult Resource Project is that, given the way in which adults are approaching those now aged 14 to 18 and are failing to perceive how they are using them and preventing them from growing up, the next generation of 18 to 24-year-olds are likely to contain more drop-outs and users of drugs, and fewer married couples grappling with the cost of living and how to get a mortgage. This can be matched with recently published figures about drug-taking in school children, which shows that between 7 and 10 per cent of secondary school children experiment with drugs [21], and the rapid increase in schoolgirl pregnancies from 0.02 per cent of total births in 1947 to 0.14 per cent in 1967 (204 to 1,240 in actual figures); this is even before the school leaving age is raised. [22] From this it is reasonable to predict the approach of a crisis which may well be overwhelming.

It is important to ask the reason for the failure of adults to be able to cope with this problem. Why are they unable to contain their own problems of anxiety, fear and stress? Why do they need to use young adults as the vehicles through which they expect these problems to be explored and dealt with and who are expected to cope with change? Insofar as the problems of the development of adolescents towards adulthood lie in the failure of adults to give a valid model of what it means to be an adult, it is reasonable to extrapolate to the hypothesis that the problems of the middle-aged (who are those likely to be most closely associated with young people) stem from their having no valid model of their own parents' generation working at the problem of growing old. As Winnicott has put it:

> "Mature adults bring vitality to that which is ancient, old and orthodox by recreating it after destroying it. And so parents move up a step, and move down a step and become grandparents." (23)

It seems that the older generation is not able to be dealt with as Winnicott suggests they should, by being tested on what they have created. Our present society believes they are either too fragile, too senile or simply irrelevant. Yet, as Cecil King pointed out in his controversial article in 'The Times':

> "Surely a dignified death is one of the greatest accomplishments — to round your life off so that you go without reluctance when the play is over. This was regarded by our ancestors as a supreme achievement, but not now."

He goes on to talk of the downgrading of birth, marriage and death and concludes:

"But to treat these events thus is to deny man dignity, purpose, and significance, for which 'economic growth' is no substitute. No wonder our young people feel they have been born into a society which is just not good enough." (24)

It is at this point that the significant contribution of the Church to the rest of society is plainly apparent. The Church is the one institution in society whose special skills and resources are called for in helping men face up to the problems of death – the pain of ending, the lost opportunities, the feelings of guilt, both on the part of the dying and those they leave behind. Interestingly enough, it was this special contribution which was perceived by all the groups of young people who met a priest, since they all spent some time talking about death with their visitor.

It may well be that, if the Church could help the old to face death maturely, the predicament of the young adult would be alleviated. This particular issue has been explored to a much greater depth by Bruce Reed in his lecture 'The Role of the Teenager'. (25)

NOTES

(1) Hansard Vol 289 No 43 Col 394
     This may, of course, be taken as an example of young people gaining from interaction with a peer.

(2) B Morris   Towards a Creative Education   New Era, Vol 49 No 3
                                                       March 1968 pp 66 and 67

(3) A Halsey,   Education, Economy and Society   The Free Press 1961
     J Floud and   Essay by J Kob - Definition of
     C Anderson   the teacher's role - p 559 ff

(4) Times Educational Supplement 22 March 1968 p 974

(5) Hansard Vol 289 No 43 Col 454

(6) Lord Soper - Col 459

(7) Lord Noel-Buxton - Col 495

(8) Op. cit p 102 and 104

(9) Op. cit p 88

(10) B Davies   Non-Swinging Youth   New Society 3 July 1969

(11) D Downes   Op. cit p 130

(12) Mark Abrams   Teenage Consumer Spending   London Press Exchange
                                                      1959

(13) Proceedings of National Association for Mental Health
     Annual Conference 1967 - Young Minds at Risk - p 13

(14) J Bugler   Puritans in Boots   New Society 13 November
                                                      1969 Vol 14 No 372 p 781

(15) M Davies   Probationers in their Social   HMSO 1969
                     Environment

(16) E M Eppel   Moral Beliefs of Young Workers,   British Journal of
                     A Comparative Study   Sociology Vol 14 1963

(17) P Willmott   Adolescent Boys in East London   Routledge and Kegan Paul 1966

(18) The Guardian 10 May 1967

(19) Quoted in The Times 13 October 1969

(20) Figures quoted in The Guardian 9 October 1969. Attributed to a confidential survey carried out by Mark Abrams for the Labour Party

(21) R S P Weiner   Drugs and Schoolchildren   Longmans 1970

(22) Figures quoted in The Times Educational Supplement 6 March 1970 p 6

(23) D Winnicott   The Family and Emotional Maturity - in The Family and Individual Development   Tavistock Publications 1965

(24) Cecil King   Depriving Man of his Dignity and Significance   The Times 9 November 1968

(25) B D Reed   The Role of the Teenager unpublished lecture   The Grubb Institute 1968

10. Common Assumptions Underlying the Planning of Work with Young Adults

The Young Adult Resource Project was set up to investigate the problems involved in helping young people make the transition to taking up full adult roles in society. It began by looking at the experience and behaviour of young people and has been forced to take more and more account of the experience and behaviour of adults, since it is understanding why adults behaved as they did which provided the key to understanding the attitudes and feelings of adolescents. In particular it showed that young people frequently experience the efforts of adults to help them, not as resources for their development but as threats against which they must seek ways of defending themselves.

Young people experience the resources of adults in this way, because adults seem to have lost a real sense of their own adulthood; thus they unconsciously use young people in different ways to help cope with this loss. Given that young people by the age of 16 or 17 have met many adults in different roles, the accumulated effect of this experience causes them to view with suspicion the institutions set up ostensibly to help them by herding them together out of touch with adult society. Their feelings about individual adults become transferred to those things seen to represent adults in general, especially those people and institutions which assume a function which focuses on 'the problems of young people'. These in their turn are then interpreted as threats to the young and not resources to help them grapple with taking up full adult roles and understanding the fundamental questions about life.

The problem can be illustrated quite simply by describing a recent incident. A group of young people mostly aged between 18 and 22 formed their own arts group. Together they experimented with ways of presenting their own poetry, music and film-making. After some time as a group they put on a public concert, mainly to raise funds, but also to present what they had been doing to a general audience. They sent complimentary tickets to a number of local figures and though only a few of those invited came, amongst them was the Deputy Mayor.

It was obvious from the start that he was puzzled by the darkness and the patterns made by the 'dream machine' shining onto the wall. He could be

97

heard talking rather loudly and nervously about 'the generation gap' and the need for people like himself to make the effort to bridge it. The concert opened with some poetry reading – much of which was hard to hear – but amongst other things the subject concerned how the writer found many things around him reminded him of death, his feelings as he contemplated making love to a girl who might not consent to his advances, the behaviour of a group of people in a pub when another customer had an epileptic fit, and finally the reactions of the Greeks to his own long-haired appearance when on holiday in their country. A trio played an item of their own composition; then a film the group had made was shown. This concerned the struggle between violence and peace which was seen to be insoluble because one extreme creates the other. The artistic quality of the different items was patchy: some of it was good, some poor, most of it mediocre. Nevertheless, the questions being explored were all made quite clear at each stage because the authors and composers explained what they were trying to get at before they performed.

At the 9 o'clock interval the Deputy Mayor was asked to speak to the audience, which he did. He started by saying that he was very pleased to be present, though he had not understood anything that had gone on. He was very happy to find so many young people enjoying themselves by being con-structive, rather than going about the streets with shaven heads and boots on. (He made no mention of long hair and demonstrations – which was as well, given the company!) He was sure that people of his age would never under-stand people of their age and vice versa but the borough council would always be keen to support local initiative like theirs. He then asked to be excused from the rest of the concert as he had a long day ahead of him and he was not as young as he used to be.

What was significant about this piece of behaviour was that the Deputy Mayor had quite clearly not recognised the questions being explored nor the fact that they had relevance to himself. It may well be reasonable that he could not understand the kinds of answers being found by the young people but the questions were largely about the problems of being human. Instead of looking at the real concern shown by these young people, he substituted a focus on the 'generation gap', presumably in the belief that this was the more important issue. In so doing he made their artistic efforts appear to be of no account in comparison, while by his behaviour he was in fact **creating** the very gap which he said he wished to bridge.

From their experience of this particular man's behaviour it would come as no surprise to find that particular arts group suspicious of any help offered it by the local council. They might well fear that it was not their art which mattered but their being young people as distinct from adults.

What is clearly illustrated by this incident is the way assumptions about young people which have lain unexamined for many years, (assumptions which may have been relevant in the past) cause a wish to be helpful to be experienced as unhelpful and even hostile.

Before proceeding to make recommendations in the light of the experience of the Young Adult Resource Project, it is important to articulate some of the assumptions which are commonly made in the planning of work with young people, because it is the assumptions made at this stage which affect what actually happens in the field. By bringing the assumptions to the surface in this way I hope that it will be possible for those engaged in planning and administering such work, especially at senior levels in voluntary and statutory services, to examine their own policies against these assumptions, if they are able to identify some of them as having influenced their decisions and policies in the light of such awareness, thus providing the basis for change.

As the assumptions underlying different kinds of work are usually taken for granted and not examined they are frequently hard to identify. Nevertheless, they subtly influence all decisions and courses of action which groups take. This is no less true in the field of work with young people. This results in very strong feelings being stirred in discussions, the resolution of which often seem to be impossible. For most people the assumptions they make when considering work with young adults spring partly from their own experience of being young and partly from their feelings about the present state of society. Maybe more importantly, they also spring from the way people feel about themselves, feelings which are projected onto young people who are then asked to deal with them. Adults are likely either to work towards reproducing something they perceive as being good for themselves, or alternatively react against what is felt to be bad for themselves. These assumptions appear to be seldom tested against reality and examined in the light of the actual needs of young people.

The following seem to be common assumptions made at the moment.

i.   Young people benefit most from interaction with those who are their own age, especially members of the opposite sex.
     This assumption appears in discussions about the size and membership of youth clubs. Many of the judgements about the quality of work done, the amount of finance given, and general statements of approval and disapproval about youth work are most easily made on this basis. It is an assumption which also influences many people's beliefs about the value of staying on at school, even though it is seldom articulated in this particular form.

ii. Young people are likely to be most helped to grow up by protecting them for as long as possible from undesirable contact with many aspects of the adult world, especially the possibility of being exploited by employers, many of whom are believed likely to be unscrupulous.

99

This is a further belief underlying the arguments for a longer school life; it sometimes takes the form of saying that young people must learn as much as possible about such things as justice, honesty and truth while they are at school because they will have little chance of learning about them once they have left and have joined the 'rat-race' of employment.

iii. **That many young people need anonymity before they can be helped to reveal their real problems to adults and receive help from them.**
Obviously much of the present trend in the development of counselling services both at school and in the local community is based on this assumption, as is evidenced by the titles of some of the services — 'Off the Record' and 'The Open Door'.

iv. **That many young people are most helped to develop emotionally in informal situations in leisuretime activities, where the problems of authority are least apparent.**
This assumption is present in the planning of all detached work and underlies a number of the community development proposals put forward in the Youth Service Development Council's recent report 'Youth and Community Work in the 70's'. [1] It is also present in much of the planning of the 'social education' of young employees and apprentices organised by industrial concerns and trade unions.

v. **That young people are basically hostile to adults, and situations need therefore to be created in which this hostility can be avoided or at least played down.**
Many current proposals which ostensibly involve young people in decision-making in different situations, from universities to youth clubs, are guided by the hope that this involvement will help overcome the hostility which is thought to be inherent in any intergenerational meeting.

vi. **That the longer young people can be encouraged to stay mainly in institutions which are educational in their intention, the better they will be helped to settle down as adult members of society.**
The increased numbers of people in full-time education, both at colleges and universities, as well as the tendency to stay on at school beyond the minimum school leaving age are the result of strong and persistent encouragement to do so. This encouragement is based on the above assumption; an assumption which has a long and honourable place in the history of education in Britain, making it that much more difficult to put it to the test. It also underlies the philosophy of present proposals to make the Youth Service more attractive to those older than most of its present membership.

vii. **That one of the problems for young people is that they are seen to be** detached from the rest of society and appear to need help to develop new attachments to it.

All work with 'unattached' young people and a great deal of other 'experimental' work, including counselling services, is planned on this assumption; it is probable that a great deal of the 'community development' approaches which arise from the YSDC report will also make this assumption.

viii. That the idealism of young people, springing from their clarity and freshness of vision and their flexibility in the face of change, should be made use of in attempting to change the nature of our modern society. This assumption is a key one to the latter half of the YSDC report but it is also made in the setting up of such bodies as Voluntary Service Overseas, Young Volunteer Force and Task Force. It has also been apparent in such public debates as the House of Lords have had on 'Youth and the Nation' and other similar topics.

To list these assumptions is not to say that any of them is necessarily wrong but to suggest that they should not be taken for granted; they need constant examination and testing in the light of experience; more than this, the fact of making them needs to be acknowledged and the possible effect calculated realistically.

Our experience in the Young Adult Resource Project indicates that the effect of making these assumptions, either individually or together, far from helping young people to make the transition to adulthood, actually hinders it. This is because the assumptions all focus the problems and difficulties, especially those concerned with effecting change, back onto the young people. In our opinion, change, if it is to be responsibly achieved, must be a feature of the behaviour of adults who seek to influence young people. This applies especially to those who may never actually encounter groups of young adults face to face, yet who set the whole tenor of the institutions in which others engage in direct relationships with them. If change is not a real part of the experience of adults, with all the grappling with uncertainty which this entails, then the change which results in young people will be brittle and short-lived or else revolutionary and uncontrolled.

This report is not the place to explore at length these assumptions and the effects of making them. This has been done to some extent by others, even in some cases using statistical methods to show when the assumptions have been made. I would refer to the work of Mr and Mrs Eppel for a fuller discussion of this. [2]

The four working hypotheses which have provided the assumptions on which this Project has been based, all related the behaviour and development of young people to the behaviour and development of adults.

These suggest that work with young people should be planned in a way which clarifies the nature of the relationship between adults and young people, in particular defining the authority that each has. This clarification enables the adults to understand their own role in a fashion which then allows the young people to learn from their own experience about the nature of both the authority they have in their own roles, and the authority of others in their roles, especially adults. To do this it is necessary for tasks, roles and boundaries to be understood, particularly by the adults. Where adults understand and accept these, they are able to give young people freedom to explore the relationship with them, both consciously and unconsciously, and to learn from this exploration

Such knowledge, and acceptance of it, is likely to help adults to have a sense of their own adulthood and an awareness of the nature of their authority as adults. This report has explored some of the factors involved in this. Clearly such an interpretation has implications for any work with young people, whatever the setting, be it educational, employment-based, in a social work or counselling situation or even in casual meetings.

To set the scene briefly for the next chapter and to contrast the Project's conclusions against the eight assumptions outlined earlier here, the key consideration in work with young adults is to focus on the adult end of the transition process. This means seeking ways of introducing young people to the world in which adults are actually engaged, not trying to create 'diluted' environments in which there are many young people but few adults – sometimes even the few there are may be uncertain of their own adulthood. The intention should be to equip the young person with assumptions about himself as a member of adult society, and help him to examine them – assumptions developed as a result of actual experience. Dr A Ryle points out in his book on student casualties, that the problem is not usually of deep-seated lack or incurable wound but that:

"... earlier experiences ... have equipped him with a set of assumptions about himself and other people which apparently limit the range of ways open to him for relating to others." (3)

The appropriate concern of policy makers should be to construct situations which ensure concentration on induction to real adult roles rather than the creation of artificial ones. Through the creation of appropriate structures those who work within them can be helped in their task of education. In the following chapter a number of specific proposals are advanced which indicate how this might be done in certain areas.

NOTES

(1) Youth Service   Youth and Community Work   HMSO 1969
     Development Council in the 70's

(2) E M and M Eppel   Adolescent Morality   Routledge and Kegan
                                                     Paul 1966

(3) A Ryle   Student Casualties   Allen Lane, the Penguin
                                                     Press 1969 p 32

11. Releasing Resources—An Assessment of Present Structures and Potentialities for Change

The previous chapter drew attention to a number of assumptions which frequently underlie and affect the planning of work with young adults, thus influencing the way work on the ground can be carried out. In particular such assumptions are made by those in senior positions in education, the Youth Service, social work and similar kinds of institution. Decisions taken and affected by such assumptions define the working situations of those who actually encounter young adults. It was suggested that the effect of making any or all of these assumptions is to create environments which, no matter how 'liberal' their intentions, actually split young people off from adult society, reduce their interaction with adults, and thus inhibit their transition to taking full adult roles themselves. The adverse effect of constructing such environments is evident not only in its failure to help young people, but also in making difficulties for the adults involved in these situations as professionals and as volunteers, subjecting them to frustration and disappointment because they are unable to help young people to the extent they would like.

The implication of all this is that work intended to help young people make the transition to taking up full adult roles needs to take place in situations which are demonstrably part of the real adult world, alongside adults who themselves understand what that means and who thus work at supporting the young adults directly in those situations, and who are in their turn supported by the structure within which they work. Supports of a specialist nature likely to be most useful to young people can then best be given through the adults who are in regular contact with young people as their employers, teachers or parents.

There are a number of important considerations to be taken when formulating recommendations following this three-year Project. In the first place there are many uncertainties about the development of educational facilities for young adults: there has been pressure for the introduction of a new Education Bill to replace the 1944 Act. Secondly, discussions have been going on of the Youth Service Development Council's Report. Thirdly there is a great deal of present examination of the place of the Youth

Employment Service in the general scheme of work with young people.
Fourthly there is the development of the social services on lines recommended
by the Seebohm Report. There are other factors which also affect the kind of
recommendations which can be made here: the developing work of the Industrial Training Boards, the changing role of the Probation and After-Care
Service, the expansion of all kinds of further education and the emergence of
a variety of different kinds of counselling services for young people. The
Young Adult Resource Project has touched on all these and the theoretical
generalisations which it has developed can be applied to each in different ways.

THE MAJOR CHANGE

It is also important to bear in mind that between the ages of 14 and 22 the
majority of young people make one of the four most important transitions
they will ever make – the transition from being educated to being employed.
(The others are from being a child at home to becoming a pupil in a school,
being single to becoming married, and being employed to being retired.) For
everyone this transition has major implications in different ways, some of
which may be perceived in advance, others of which can only be discovered
through experience. The Young Adult Resource Project has attempted to
identify what bodies exist to offer support through this transition and how that
support is used.

Though some of the work, both through formal and informal settings, has
been done with those who have gone on to higher education or into comparatively
high status jobs such as the Civil Service and the printing trade, the majority
of my time and energy has been spent with those who left school at 15 and went
into unskilled and semi-skilled employment, or even into lengthy periods of
unemployment. It is with the interests of these latter young people mainly in
mind that this chapter is written, particularly given the general failure to
date to understand and grapple with the problems which they represent.
Nevertheless, the experience of this Project indicates that the problems
especially brought to light by such young people are also experienced by their
more able contemporaries who are also involved in the same transition,
though the nature of the difficulty is frequently obscured for various reasons.

The fundamental problem for them all, lies in the virtual non-existence
of the kind of support which would enable work at the attachments and
commitments (in Goffman's sense) which they already have to different parts
of adult society.

The services usually assumed to be supports – for example youth work
activities or counselling services – frequently distract attention from the
areas where the problems of transition can be identified most clearly. In
place of heightened awareness of those real difficulties, substitutes are
established which increase the complexity of the situation without adding to

the resources to help grapple with the issues. The reason for the failure to increase the resources, is that such additional structures not only may distract the young people from the process of taking up full adult roles, but they also cause considerable difficulties for the adults who work within them. Adults find themselves split off from the rest of the adult world, occupying a kind of adolescent limbo, unsupported in the business of their own development. Because the adults themselves are distracted in this way, they are likely to find it difficult to provide a clear model to young people of what it means to take a full adult role in society.

What has been evident in this Project is that it is those adults taking roles clearly seen to have a real function in society, who find it most easy to make their personal resources available to young people. Their own sense of confidence about their role, not simply that they feel comfortable in it, but rather that they recognise the value of grappling with the problems the role presents, is a feature which is appreciated by young people and evokes constructive responses from them. This provides a sense of dependability which gives young people freedom to relate to the adult in a realistic fashion – exploring affinities and differences, and accepting or rejecting what is offered without a sense of guilt or obligation, thus allowing them to get on with the business of their own development for themselves.

This has two important implications for considering the kinds of organisation and structures which are likely to help or hinder young people in their development towards maturity.

i. Structures intended to help young people, need to provide them with opportunities of interacting with adults who understand their own roles in society and are able to maintain this understanding in their dealings with young people.

ii. The young people themselves need to have available to them, roles which are not exclusively taken by young people. This provides them with models of adults taking the same role as themselves, enabling them to begin to make distinctions between the authority related to that role and authority which arises from experience – the authority of adulthood.

It has not been the function of this Project to examine in detail the individual structures which exist at present to help young people in their transition to adulthood. This means that most of the comments which can be made are of a rather general nature, intending to draw attention to a principle rather than to suggest specific alterations or innovations.

What emerges most importantly is the need for a change of emphasis in the way people think about supporting young people in transition. At present, thinking is often dominated by the belief that the best help can be offered through 'leisure-time' activities. The overwhelming evidence of this Project

105

is that this is mistaken. It is through young people's work or their family life that resources can be made most available for their use. This means that those in the best position to help young people are their employers, their parents and their teachers, supported in their turn by the Youth Employment Service, the Industrial Training Boards and other specialists who may be called on to assist. These specialists will include the local church, counsellors of various kinds and the Youth Service.

THE YOUTH EMPLOYMENT SERVICE

It has been evident in this Project that mature behaviour has been most consistently displayed by young people at their place of work. This has been clear whether they have been in unskilled work or highly skilled, whether they came from the lowest streams of comprehensive schools or had been through sixth forms and were following courses of higher education. It has been in their role as employees that young adults have been better able to tolerate uncertainty and stress, to explore differences, and to think through issues with visitors to the groups. Visitors to groups of young employees have regularly commented on their intelligence and good sense – even when the young people concerned have left school at 15 and gone into unskilled employment. This indicates that of all the situations explored in this Project, that of employment has been the one where young people have been best able to use help in finding out what it means to be an adult, because they have been best able to use their own resources with a sense of freedom.

What is clearly called for, therefore, is a service which is equipped to support young people in this most important area of their lives.

The Youth Employment Service is strategically the most significant body at present available to give this support to young people at this stage, because it has links with young people both at school and at work.

This is not to suggest in any way that the Service, as at present organised and thought about, fully appreciates the significance or the nature of its potential contribution to the development of young adults. The 1965 Albemarle Report on the Service [1] commented on its low morale and made some suggestions about how this might be improved, but quite overlooked many of the possibilities which actually exist. The two current documents from the Department of Employment and Productivity and the Central Youth Employment Executive [2] both share the same weakness in that neither of them examine in any depth the importance of the unique situation which the Youth Employment Service occupies.

In recent years efforts have been made to improve the kind of work done in schools. Exhibitions, careers conventions, direct work in classrooms as well as the development of liaison work with careers teachers have all increased in importance. But the point of focus of all this has remained the choice of the first job and preparation for that, including choices about further education where necessary.

What is called for is a new conception of the work of the Service which focuses not on placement (or even preparation for placement) but upon the long term problem of making the transition from education to employment.

This four-year study has demonstrated young adults' need and willingness to explore and develop their understanding of the roles to which they are committed and attached, and the necessity to do this through interaction with adults who can give young people freedom to carry out this exploration because they themselves understand and accept their roles. It is therefore necessary for the Youth Employment Service to develop new approaches and understanding of its work, which break quite new and potentially very fertile ground by taking these needs into account. In the first place such approaches could be designed to liberate the resources of young people, of teachers and of employers to grapple with these issues in which they are all involved because of their common situation. Yet value needs to be given to the different interests and points of view which need to be related to each other, rather than denied or irrevocably separated. This calls for a Service which is basically an educational service with its educational function relating to adults as well as to young people, to those in employment as well as to those in schools and colleges. Careers advisory officers in such a service would need to be at least as involved with employers and teachers as with young people, and giving at least as much time to those in their first two years of employment as to those in their last year or so in education.

By focusing on the total process of the transition from education to employment it would soon become apparent that for many young people it would be important to return from employment to full-time education for a period. As things stand at the moment, many of those who left school at the age of 15 have a strong desire to return to school or college two years later, believing that their experience of employment would enable them to make much better use of being back in education. Yet few are able to do this. At the present moment few suitable courses exist; those which exist do not get wide general publicity because they would not be able to cope with the demand for places if they were more widely publicised. But more important than publicity, the vast majority of 17-year-olds at work never get the encouragement to consider going back to full-time education because they do not come in contact with people who either recognise their need or help them consider it seriously. A careers advisory officer involved with young people over periods of five years or more would be in a position to help them work this question out at the point in their lives when it mattered to them. The Service as a whole would also be in a strong position to mobilise pressure for the provision of appropriate courses.

In order to be able to focus on the whole question of transition, with its possible movements between education and employment, which might be repeated two or even three times by any one individual, the present upper age limit of 18 or being in full-time school education is probably inappropriate to the service. To carry out its task properly it would have to be responsible for all young people between the ages of 14 and 24. This would then cover all those who decide to take their education up to degree level and probably include their first 18 months or so at work. By being responsible for and involved with young people over this length of time, careers advisory officers would be guarded from being insignificant figures existing on the fringes of schools, who flit through a 20 minute interview with 14-year-olds to be forgotten a few months later, but would be in a position to develop an expertise and specialism which would be of great importance both to teachers and employers, as well as to young people themselves. This would bring the advisory officer into a more realistic relationship with both these groups of adults.

By approaching the work of the Service in this way it becomes possible to see that what is envisaged is not a peripheral service to education, but in fact is the lynch-pin around which this major changeover in the lives of young people can be built, thus enabling it to take place as smoothly as possible, while providing the maximum opportunities for all concerned to use their resources constructively and to learn from their own contributions to the process. It would provide the basis for the service's own flexibility, which would enable employers, teachers and young people themselves to be as flexible as possible through this stage without sacrificing the stability important to providing support for the young people in transition. Given the fact that change is one major phenomenon in modern society, any structures created to help young people need to be set up recognising the probability of themselves being subject to change. This in its own turn would better fit those who work within such structures to prepare others for change. [3]

The constant factor to be borne in mind is not solely the need to provide a vast range of experiences for young people but to find ways of helping them to interpret new experiences in relation to their previous experience and the general process of transition in which they are engaged. Further, it is important to add that this Project has shown that the most significant people to help in this are not outsiders but the actual teachers and employers whom young people encounter in the day-to-day situation. Careers advisory officers are agents to support the adults in their work, not to take over from them.

This conception of the Service — flexible, involving teachers, employers, trades unionists and young people — working with an eye on the passage of time rather than reacting to immediate situations without consideration for the past or the future — depends on the belief that there is a general desire on the part of all concerned, that the transition from being educated to being employed shall be carried out in a way which liberates people's resources for more effective use. It is clearly to the advantage of employers to have young people better prepared for their work; it is in the interests of teachers that young people leave school having made the best use of the opportunities available to them; it is in the interests of young people that they make this major changeover in their lives, in the best way possible. The behaviour of young people I have met during this Project and described in this report, (as well as that described by others such as the Eppels) makes it clear that young people in general want this. The question which is clearly posed is whether or not adults in general want it. It is through their pressure for change, that the structures which enable a better transition can be created.

The kind of Service which has been envisaged here is clearly not a youth **employment** service. Though it requires an Act of Parliament (or at least an amendment to one) to change that name, I would suggest that this service be named, the Education and Employment Advisory Service, and its officers simply called Advisory Officers. The Service should be realistically staffed, not as in the present situation where in many areas there are more youth leaders and counsellors than there are careers advisory officers, indicating a clear value judgement about the perceived importance of each service at the present moment.

Finally, it is worth making the point that an Education and Employment Advisory Service such as that described, would have a major part to play in the development of work in schools. At the present moment schools easily become inward looking, even if not just inward to themselves; they still often judge their success and acquire kudos through passing people further on inside the educational system, to higher education of one sort or another. By giving them a major link with employment with strength and imaginative approaches, the Education and Employment Advisory Service would enrich the life of the school and open up the range of opportunities seen to be available when people leave.

SCHOOLS AND FURTHER EDUCATION

The overall structure

The evidence of this Project causes some of the assumptions which underlie the present conception of secondary and further education to be open to question. The most important of these is the common belief that a longer school career is likely to help young people to develop more quickly towards maturity. This is a major assumption underlying the policy of raising the school-leaving age. The longer school career – secondary education for all – is an honoured objective of much liberal thinking about education for nearly a century and any criticism of it as a policy must be made with the greatest possible caution.

109

Nevertheless my experience of the last three and a half years strongly suggests that behaviour of young people in the educational settings of schools and college is in general less mature than that of people in employment settings.

This was not a function of ability, vanboys and warehousemen behaved in ways which displayed greater freedom and confidence in meeting adults than those working for University Entrance and academic qualifications. Because they were more experienced in close, continuing relationships with adults in their every day situation they were able to criticise, accept and reject the views and attitudes of the visitors with a degree of selectivity. The young people from school and college either absorbed or rejected what they were presented with in an almost uncritical fashion. One way of interpreting why this happened is to point out that in school and college the differences of role between student and teacher coincide with generational differences, whereas at work most young employees will have adults as colleagues carrying out broadly the same role as themselves. Thus the very structure of a school or college makes all its members vulnerable to the frustrations and difficulties which are described in Chapter 3 of this report. What is called for is a structure where differences in roles do not have this coincidence, where some adults take the same role as young people as well as some taking different ones.

The work of this Project leads me to believe that this talent could be better developed, along with the personal and moral qualities of people whatever their academic ability, if compulsory full-time schooling were not to extend beyond 15. In fact there is a serious case to be made that it might even be lowered so that the actual decision about staying or leaving is taken earlier. That is to say, the choice about remaining at school or leaving would be taken earlier, thus enabling young people to take real responsibility for themselves sooner than when this choice is taken for them by force of law. In order to make the choice one which is reasonable it would be worth considering the possibility of paying people to stay at school. This would help them compare what school really has to offer them against work.

Such a scheme could not be justified without being considered in a fully educational context. To focus one's whole educational career at this very early age, to then leave school and to go directly into employment without further contact with the education system would be to encourage the loss of talent feared by the Crowther Committee. It would also make the provision of developing courses in schools almost impossible. The decision to leave school at 14 or so should be followed by the compulsory part-time education which is already on the Statute Book, not only in the 1944 Education Act but also the 1918 Education Act. The purpose of this compulsory part-time release up to the age of 18, would be to help clarify the experience of young people in the first instance and then to find ways of helping them gain the information and skills they need as a result of their own assessment of the situation. Such work could only be done meaningfully in consultation with Industrial Training Boards, officers of the suggested Education and Employment Advisory Service, teachers and employers (especially the latter), because the young people will best be able to use their experience of being at college when they are aware of the nature of the authority given them by their employers when they attend. This will help them be more aware of the adult part of their role as students and help them avoid regressing and behaving as if their role were the same as that of a pupil in a school.

The form of the part-time education could range from the half-day release twice a week which is laid down in the 1944 Education Act, through to whole days and block release for a variety of periods. It should also be possible to return to full-time education either at school or in college. In fact the single most effective way of helping schools approach the problems of preparing young people to take their place in adult society, would be to have amongst its students those who have left school for a period and have then chosen to return to do studies of different kinds. Such returners could have been at work for 2 to 3 years but could also well be people who are older, such as mothers whose own children have reached school-age and who now wish to take up their own formal education again. Colleges could well include people in mid-career taking specialist courses of different kinds. Such adults, taking the role of students alongside young people, would provide models of how adults take such a role. The more significant the courses to the adults' own career, the more seriously he would take his life in college, the greater resource he would be to students younger than himself.

In this context the significance of the role of the Education and Employment Advisory Service can again be clearly seen because its work would be continuous and would focus on a recognition that work (not just a job) is a central factor in an individual's life and his developing conception of himself. It has already been pointed out that the Service would be in the position to provide the support and the environment which could enable decisions about staying in one job, changing it or returning to education, to be taken in the most responsible way. Thus, even the act of making different decisions can be used as an opportunity for learning and development because it is carried out in conjunction with the support of an experienced adult adviser.

The classroom situation

What emerges from this Project is the importance of helping teachers to be more aware of the dynamics of group situations. What has been evident in the teachers who have visited groups has been a sensitivity to these dynamics but an inability to use them creatively because their instinct has been to defend themselves against them. The sensitivity they have had has meant that the defences used have been very effective. Thus the teachers' sensitivity has usually caused them to be unhelpful to the young people they have met.

In their preliminary training teachers need to be helped to develop an understanding of this sensitivity to what is happening in groups which they can then learn to use constructively when they are in schools. This sort of training has been pioneered by Elizabeth Richardson in Bristol University in recent years but needs to be much more widely used than at present. [4]

What is also important is that teachers need to develop a much greater awareness of themselves as the representatives of the whole of the school staff group when they are in a classroom, to recognise the nature of their authority as members of that group. Regular staff meetings working at real issues can provide some genuine feeling about this so long as such meetings are able to be more than simply platforms for the head teacher to address his subordinates. Proper supervision of teachers in their probationary year applying the model of casework supervision used by social workers is another way of working at the same issue. [5]

A problem which continually faces schools is a tendency towards encapsulation: the teacher tends to become encapsulated in the classroom and the classroom in the school. The process in which the growing child is involved is one of moving outwards, cutting through this encapsulation. For teachers to be able to help this process as it develops, they must be involved in it themselves all the time. They must develop work in conjunction with the local community, not simply in leisure activities but more importantly with local industry, and further education. The Education and Employment Advisory Service working on lines suggested earlier in the chapter could represent a significant resource to help teachers to do this.

In recent years very important developments have occurred in the understanding of what is meant by the managing of different kinds of enterprise. Because this involves relating the internal world of a group to its environment, it provides a way of avoiding the kind of encapsulation mentioned above. To help teachers to understand more about the management of educational situations and to learn to think of themselves as managers would therefore be important. More than that, because management is such a central feature of all organised life in modern society, the observation and understanding of how schools are managed could provide pupils with a way of looking at the world beyond school which would be extremely valuable as they think about their future occupations.

But in the end what has been evident in this Project has been that adults, including teachers, can be no better than the structure to which they belong. What is called for is a major attack on the problem of applying modern approaches to management organisation to schools; in particular understanding the nature of the key role in the school, that of the head teacher.

EMPLOYERS AND THE INDUSTRIAL TRAINING BOARDS

If further education to the age of 18 is made compulsory then employers and the Industrial Training Boards will have to take the problems of the semi-and unskilled employee more seriously than they have yet done. Their involvement with colleges will be crucial because the colleges are seldom equipped by experience or even attitude, to know how to approach the education of such young people. Because of local variations, what is probably called for is joint working by individual colleges with the actual firms in their area, not simply the creation of a national syllabus and approach.

The fundamental point is that if employers, Industrial Training Boards and educationists are between them unable to work out ways of understanding what it means to be a semi- or unskilled employee in their firms, they cannot expect their young employees to understand it either. Further than this they cannot expect their own young employees to respond at all creatively to the opportunities with which they are presented. This would provide an important stimulus for re-examining many of the jobs which exist at the moment in order to make them more meaningful in the long run.

Often this may mean total restructuring of a number of jobs; but it may also mean looking at an existing job in a new light. For example, many van-boys work with driver-salesmen, that is to say their lorries do not carry pre-arranged orders to customers but are effectively travelling shops. Such van-boys can be seen realistically, not as labour to help carry loads, but as trainee and assistant salesmen. Looked at in this light, a number of different things of an educational nature could be planned, which would make a job, currently seen as dead-end, the introduction to a particular skill capable of being developed throughout one's working life.

So far the Industrial Training Act operating on its own has not forced the attention of employers and trainers on this significant area of employment which it was actually meant to influence. If part-time education to 18 were compulsory and the provisions of the Industrial Training Act continued, real progress could be made in this vital area.

This three-pronged approach to the problems of the greater part of the school leaving population represents the only way of tackling them with any hope of success. If this approach is not developed the contributions of their services will inevitably be disjointed and uncertain; a few individuals may be helped but provision for the bulk of young adults will remain non-existent. The recommendations which make up the remainder of this chapter are only coherent in the light of what has been said so far.

THE YOUTH SERVICE

The distinctive contribution of the Youth Service, in whatever form it takes, is that it provides ways of using informal settings within which adults and young people can interact, especially during their leisure-time. But in its very distinctiveness lies the Service's greatest handicaps. These are:

i.   its being a leisure-time service;

ii.   its 'informality' easily obscures the importance of tasks and roles, and thus makes it hard for adults to recognise how to stay in role and thus to be of use to young people in their development.

By offering a leisure-based service the youth worker is inevitably competing with all the alternative occupations which may call upon a young person's time: his family, his work and his friends. In the long run these, especially the first two, will be more important than most youth work can realistically expect to be. The constant difficulty is that, below the level of consciousness, the youth worker feels that because his livelihood depends on young people, they have a reciprocal dependence upon him. Obviously this is not the case when looked at rationally and no one would argue that it should be. Nevertheless it is easily felt and then communicated by behaviour.

If the tasks, roles and boundaries in youth work were clearer, there would be opportunities for adults to become more fully aware of their own behaviour, and its implications for what young people learn. But seldom are these factors clearly articulated, especially where work is carried out in settings like coffee bars, discotheques and detached work. The problem arises because a youth worker in a coffee bar may feel that he has two conflicting tasks – as a coffee bar or discotheque manager, and as a youth worker – tasks he may be uncertain how to reconcile. The result of this is that the adults involved are likely to respond to the pressures put on them by young people either by abdicating as adults or by behaving in authoritarian ways. What is put at risk by working in these ill-defined settings is the capacity to use those self-same pressures to help learning and development. It is failure to use the inevitable testing of adults by the young people for learning, which causes the resources offered by adults to be experienced as threats. It was because of the loss of opportunities to explore what it means to be approaching full adult status, which I became aware of in the first few months, that I evolved the group method which became the basis of this Project. One session in a group provided more opportunities which could be used for learning than appeared in two months of walking the streets of Islington.

A further problem for the Youth Service also stems from its lack of defined tasks. The expectations held of the Youth Service by other parts of society frequently are that it will contribute to tackling the problem of rising delinquency, increasing drug-taking, petty vandalism and the anti-authority attitudes of young people. Many of these expectations are more likely to be met effectively in other areas of the lives of young people than their leisure-time. But because the Youth Service is felt by those who work within it to

114

have a low status, there is an inevitable desire to be thought well of and thus a temptation to collude with attempting the impossible. Unfortunately senior members of the Service are likely to be even more active in encouraging this sort of collusion than those who in face-to-face involvement with young people, attempt to carry out the policies which are laid upon them. The danger of this is that people's integrity may frequently be sorely tested.

It follows from this that the Youth Service, both as at present generally constituted, and also as envisaged by the Youth Service Development Council's recent report, cannot realistically represent a major contribution to the development of young people as they take up full adult roles. This is not to deny the help it does give but to guard against inflating that contribution and the danger of it absorbing more resources than it actually justifies. Whatever contribution it does make can only be realistically judged insofar as it supports the contributions made by the major structures in which young people are involved, their schools or colleges, their work and their families. This provides an argument for associating youth work with these structures but it must be done in a way which relates to their task and not be carried out in a way which splits young people off from them. The ultimate success of youth work can therefore be seen in terms of the extent to which it is able to help young people to settle into those institutions constructively. If the Youth Service does anything else it appears to young people as a form of bribe to distract attention from these basic parts of society. If this happens, the Service in whatever form it takes will be seen as threatening rather than as a resource to young people wishing to take their full place in society.

THE CHURCHES

When the Young Adult Resource Project was initially conceived it was intended that part of its function would be to examine the contribution of the churches to the development of young adults. In fact this has developed in the Project in an unexpected way.

When I was working at setting up the Project, I was unable to find a method of relating local churches to it. This was primarily because of the Project's relation with the EWR Club which caused local clergy to see what I was doing mainly in youth club terms. Since they already had various forms of youth work of their own, whatever I represented was seen as being beyond what their churches were intended to do, or indeed had the resources for. This has meant that no continuing work has been done with any individual church.

It has not, therefore, been possible to observe the attitudes of young people towards any one particular church, and in some ways this is a serious disadvantage. However, what it was possible to observe was how young people have reacted to the prospect of meeting a priest and how they behaved when they met one. From this it is possible to infer tentatively certain things about young people and churches in general.

Of the fourteen groups taken, five asked to meet a priest. In each of the five cases there was a sense of some daring when the suggestion was made and there was always more debate about asking a priest than any other visitor. In one group it was finally decided not to go ahead with the invitation, so in the end four groups actually met a minister.

In all of them, up to the week of the visit, there were occasional attempts to change the decision, none of which was carried through. In one way their fear was articulated as being afraid of being 'got at' or 'preached at', though their behaviour at this point indicated that what was more important was their belief that what a person might have to say to them was unlikely to be very relevant to their own lives. But even this view never appeared to me to be held with real conviction and it seemed necessary to find some other interpretation of their behaviour.

This became apparent following reflection upon how the young people actually behaved in relation to the priests they met and the kind of questions they asked.

When the visitors came, the issues which they raised all concerned major points in human life: birth, marriage and death. The questions which were asked showed the young people's anxiety about the meaning of the world and their own lives in it. Their unspoken belief was that the contribution of the churches was to help them understand these issues. The pressure which all the clergy experienced was on one hand to resist being swamped by the young people's problems, and on the other to be able to demonstrate their Christian faith without 'preaching', to relate their theology to the problems the young people were presenting without making the young people feel that they ought to belong to a church. Of the four priests, one was swamped by the power of the young people's feelings about the issues raised; one went through an hour-and-a-half without specifically mentioning God once; a third resorted to an analysis of the theological basis of Henry VIII's split with Rome; and the fourth has already been described as having managed to hold together his beliefs and the problems presented to him in a way which was appreciated by the young people.

It seems that what these priests (and therefore their churches) represented in prospect to these young people was the opportunity to work at issues which raised considerable anxiety for them. These were issues which they were almost too frightened to look at, yet which were raised simply by being made aware of the churches' existence. This was evident in people's behaviour before ever a priest came to a group.

The demand that was made of the visiting priests by these young people was to understand the real nature of the young people's anxieties and to offer the resources of the churches to grapple with those anxieties as young people experience them. What the young people feared was that they would simply be told to go to church or be evangelised in a way which might appear to be much the same thing to them. What they were really wanting in the first place was an answer to whether or not the world in general was a place which could be trusted, a place in which one could be exposed to seeming chaos without being destroyed by it. The powerful impact of the priest who visited the van-boys arose from the fact that he demonstrated by his behaviour that he believed that it was. This meant that he could expose himself to the world with confidence in ways which were at first sight apparently fraught with risk. To infer the role of the churches from how (a) these young people wanted to use their representatives; and (b) an understanding of the resources of the churches, would suggest a conclusion along the following lines.

Young adults, on the verge of taking up full adult roles in society, are inevitably anxious about the meaning of those roles and the tasks which they will undertake, they are uncertain about the long-term purpose of their own and other people's lives. They are aware of the chaos of the world they are about to join and many of them are very frightened of it and afraid of exposing themselves to it.

This situation in which the young adult finds himself is one in which he is aware of chaos both inside and outside himself. Where this chaos overwhelms him he will seek a variety of means of escape.

The specific contribution of the Church is to help people to recognise that if they believe that the world is under the authority of God, is part of His Kingdom, it will be experienced as a sufficiently dependable place for them to take the risks necessary for living creatively within it. To do this the Church must be able to help people to tolerate the anxiety which is involved in taking those risks. The Church's most important message to young people today is that God can be trusted and Christians need to be able to demonstrate this in their own behaviour.

This is a different message from the one which young people believe that they are getting from the Church. What they think they hear is that the only institution in the world which can be trusted is the Church. They think they know from their own experience (or at least the experience of their parents) that this is not the case. It is because they think that this is the Church's message that many young people cope with their present despair by turning to drugs and searching oriental philosophies for alternative sources of hope. These searches are effectively a vote of no confidence in the Church.

To be able to make some impact on this calls for a recognition by churches of the wider boundaries of the communities within which they exist and their own role within those boundaries. In the past the churches pioneered a great deal of what has now become the Youth Service; they need to do this no longer because the problems of young people will not be met appropriately by the churches through the provision of structures which split them off from the older generation. In fact, the churches through their ordinary services of worship can provide a situation in which people of all ages can take part together on an equal basis as worshippers. When services are devised and conducted in such ways as to help congregations to experience and contemplate their dependence upon God, worshippers will be able to 'go out into the world with faith' and take up their roles in it in the knowledge that it is a place which can ultimately be trusted, no matter how much one may experience anxiety and stress in it.

The provision of youth clubs, coffee bars and discotheques can only be seen as bribes of one sort or another which suppress anxiety and thus make the distinctive contribution of the local church more difficult to discern by young people and to use for themselves. One service which might appropriately be offered by churches would be a counselling service for parents of adolescents.

COUNSELLING SERVICES FOR PARENTS AND FAMILIES

Figuring high in the kinds of problems being presented at young people's counselling services have been relations with parents. The effect of contacts between parents and teachers in terms of improved performance by young people and their greater happiness, has been fully explored in the Plowden and Newsom Reports [6 and 7] and by Dr J W B Douglas. [8] In her report on the first NAYC project with unattached youth, Mary Morse [9] drew attention to the extent to which parents were concerned about their adolescent sons and daughters and commented that much could be done through family counselling services.

During the course of this Project a number of adults visiting groups have indicated that they would themselves value some form of advice centre to help them cope with the stresses of being parents of adolescents. For many of these, their children were unlikely to become delinquent or to be socially deprived in the ordinary sense; they did not, therefore, regard themselves as needing the help of the normal social agencies. What they sought was a setting within which to receive support and guidance in working at the complex problems of changing their relationships with their children in response to their growing up.

At the present moment there is a strong tendency to wish to deal with young people without taking account of the authority of their parents. The consequence can easily become a form of tug-of-war in which the young adult becomes the victim of seemingly divergent forces which exploit his own ambivalence about the process of separating himself off from his family. It is unlikely that he will experience much freedom if this happens in such a process.

He would be more helped if his parents were assisted in working at their own problems of changing their role in relation to him, learning to understand their own authority and how to use it, as well as encouraging him to do the same. To work at the issue in this way would encourage parents to have greater respect for themselves rather than feeling that they were irrelevant, ill-informed and old-fashioned.

Work of this nature would be best done in groups of both mothers and fathers, exploring the different issues which concern each of them. They would be most helped in this by having the aid of a consultant who should encourage attempts to get at and understand the nature of the problem rather than simply seek speedy solutions. In terms of helping the adolescent off-spring, more is likely to result from the parents' trying to understand the issues, rather than their having answers to questions which might be used defensively. The greatest benefit will spring from a developing capacity in parents to recognise stress and to tolerate it.

A number of different bodies besides local churches might offer a service of this nature. It might be offered through Parent-Teacher Associations in secondary schools or colleges, or through Marriage Guidance Councils.

SOCIAL WORK

This Project is an educational one and not a therapeutic one. Much (though by no means all) of what social workers have to do is of a therapeutic nature. This means that such people as child care officers and probation officers make some assumptions as they work which are different from those made by teachers and youth leaders. They also make some which are common to both fields. For this reason it was possible for me to work with probation officers and child care officers in this Project. But the differences between education and therapy mean that any recommendations made here must be made cautiously.

It has been evident that the concepts of authority, task, role and boundaries as they have been described and used in this Project have proved helpful tools to the social workers with whom I have been involved. This suggests that the exploration of these concepts, including learning how to use them to illuminate one's own experience, should constitute part of the training of social workers. Further than this, what is suggested is that those in more senior posts in social work organisations should be better equipped as managers of their institutions. This would make them better able to help their subordinates learn to exercise their authority more judiciously and thus to be more supportive to their young adult clients.

Because of the sensitivity to human needs which social work training focuses on, and because teachers have to learn to exercise authority if they are to survive in the classroom, a powerful case has been made by Professor

Tibble for some years for areas of joint training for both teachers and social workers. Already some colleges of education are involved in doing this but it is a practice which should be extended because of the long-term benefit to both professions.

What must be recognised is the fact that this training leads ultimately to two different professions carrying out different tasks in society. To amalgamate some parts of their training should not be seen as an opportunity to obliterate important differences between the two.

CONCLUSION

In the end the problem which has emerged as central has been to create ways in which young people can take a place in adult society, not creating special young people's areas in which adults can find a place, but finding ways of helping them to be alongside adults and to take a full part in an adult situation. To create special settings for young adults, no matter how enjoyable or well thought out these might be, is simply to split young people off into a world of their own, inevitably a world of unreality – as the boy quoted in the opening page of the Newsom Report said, 'It could be all marble, Sir, but it would still be a bloody school'. To do this means that all those adults who come into contact with young people, as colleagues at work, in educational and social situations, will each become responsible for making some contribution to their development. This will call for a capacity to face the fundamental questions posed by young people – not answering them for others, but grappling with the questions each one for himself. The most significant resource available to every young adult is the model of how a mature person faces up to and persists in working at those questions which challenge him most deeply. Where adults fail to do this then we prove ourselves unworthy of being depended upon, failing to provide the leadership needed to help young people take up their places as members of adult society, able in their turn to cope with the stresses and the uncertainties which this involves. It comes as no surprise therefore to find young people seeking alternatives on which to depend and these are not necessarily better than what they are turning from – drugs, oriental religions or sexual activity. The behaviour of young people is a reflection back to the adult world of itself – young people are the writing on our wall.

NOTES

(1) The Future Development of the Youth Employment Service HMSO 1965

(2) Central Youth Employment Executive   The Future Structure of the Youth Employment Service   HMSO 1970

Department of Employment and Productivity   The Future of the Employment Services – A consultative document   DEP 1970

(3) Some ideas about approaches have been put forward by Dr M E M Herford, an Appointed Factory Doctor. See:

M E M Herford   Medical Care and Vocational   The British Hospital and
                Guidance   Social Service Journal
                                              August 1964

M E M Herford   A View of Medicine   Transactions of the Society
                                              of Occupational Medicine
                                              Vol 17 No 4 1967

(4) For descriptions of this training and its application to schools see:
E Richardson   Group Study for Teachers   Routledge and Kegan Paul
                                              1967
E Richardson   The Environment of Learning   Nelson 1967
E Richardson   The staff group and its problems Lecture to the British
                of authority and shared   Association for the Advan-
                responsibility   cement of Science 1968

(5) I Caspari and   Supervising School Practice   The New Era Vol 48,
     S J Eggleston   No 6 June 1967

(6) Children and their Primary Schools — Report of the Central Advisory
     Council for Education HMSO 1966

(7) Half Our Future — Report of the Central Advisory Council for
     Education HMSO 1963

(8) J W B Douglas   Home and School   McGibbon and Kee 1965

(9) M Morse   The Unattached   Pelican 1965
     see also
     J B Mays   Growing up in the City   Liverpool University
                                               Press 1956

Bibliography

Abrams, M. (1959) Teenage Consumer Spending. London Press Exchange
Albermarle (1965) The Future Development of the Youth Employment
   Service. HMSO
Barnard, R. (1968) Initiation by Violence - the uses of Delinquency.
   New Society, 27.6.68
Bion, W. R. (1961) Experiences in Groups. Tavistock Publications
Blishen, Edward (1966) Roaring Boys. Panther
Bugler, J. (1969) Puritans in Boots. New Society, 13.11.69
Burton, G. (1965) People Matter More than Things. Hodder
Carter, M. (1966) Into Work. Pelican
Caspari, I. and Eggleston, S. J. (1967) Supervising School Practice.
   The New Era, 48, No. 6
Central Youth Employment Executive (1970) The Future Structure of the
   Youth Employment Service. HMSO
Crowther, G. (1959) 15-18, Report of the Central Advisory Council for
   Education. HMSO
Davies, B. (1969) Non-Swinging Youth. New Society, 3.7.69
Davies, M. (1969) Probationers in their Social Environment. HMSO
Department of Employment and Productivity (1970) Future of the Employment
   Service - Consultative Document. DEP
Douglas, J. W. B. (1965) Home and School. McGibbon and Kee
Downes, D. (1966) The Delinquent Solution. Routledge and Kegan Paul
Eppel, E. M. (1963) Moral Beliefs of Young Workers - a comparative study.
   British Journal of Sociology, 14
Eppel, E. M. (1967) The Adolescent Predicament. National Association for
   Mental Health
Eppel, E. M. and Eppel, M. (1966) Adolescents and Morality. Routledge
   and Kegan Paul
Erikson, E . (1967) Identity, Youth in Crisis. Faber and Faber
Goetschius, G. W. and Tash, J. (1967) Working with Unattached Youth.
   Routledge and Kegan Paul
Goffman, E. (1969) Where the Action Is. Allen Lane, The Penguin Press
Hamblett, C. and Deverson, J. (1964) Generation X. Sphere Books
Hart, H. L. A. (1969) The Report of the Committee on Relations with
   Junior Members. Oxford University Press
Herford, M. E. M. (1964) Medical Care and Vocational Guidance.
   The British Hospital and Social Service Journal, August 1964
Herford, M. E. M. (1967) A View of Medicine. Transactions of the Society
   of Occupational Medicine, 17, No. 4
Houghton, V. P. (1970) The Myth of Intergenerational Conflict. University
   of Nottingham Education Paper No. 11
Jephcott, P. (1967) Time of One's Own. Oliver and Boyd
King, C. (1968) Depriving Man of his Dignity and Significance.
   The Times, 9.11.68

Kob, J. (1961) Definition of the Teacher's Role in Education Economy and
    Society. (Ed) Halsey, Floud and Anderson. The Free Press
Laurie, Peter (1965) Teenage Revolution. Blond
McInnes, Colin (1964) Absolute Beginners. Penguin
Merton, R. K. (1957) Social Theory and Social Structure. The Free Press
Miller, E. J. and Rice, A. K. (1967) Systems of Organization.
    Tavistock Publications
Morris, B. (1968) Towards a Creative Education. The New Era, **49**, No.3
Morse, Mary (1965) Unattached. Pelican
Musgrove, F. (1964) Youth and the Social Order. Routledge and Kegan Paul
Newsom, J. (1963) Half our Future - Report of the Central Advisory
    Council for Education. HMSO
Northrop Frye (1963) The University and Personal Life in Higher Education,
    Demand and Response. (Ed) W. R. Niblett. Tavistock Publications
Plowden (1966) Children and their Primary Schools - Report of the Central
    Advisory Council for Education. HMSO
Reed, B. D. (1968) The Role of the Teenager (unpublished lecture).
    The Grubb Institute of Behavioural Studies
Rice, A. K. (1963) The Enterprise and its Environment. Tavistock
    Publications
Rice, A. K. (1965) Learning for Leadership. Tavistock Publications
Richardson, E. (1967) The Environment of Learning. Nelson
Richardson, E. (1967) Group Study for Teachers. Routledge and Kegan Paul
Richardson, E. (1968) The Staff Group and Its Problems of Authority and
    Shared Responsibility. Lecture to British Association for the Advance-
    ment of Science, August 1968
Ryle, A. (1969) Student Casualties. Allen Lane, The Penguin Press
Schofield, M. (1965) The Sexual Behaviour of Young People. Longmans
Studt, E. (1966) Worker-client Authority Relationships in Social Work -
    in 'New Developments in Casework' (Ed) E. Younghusband.
    National Institute for Social Work Training
Welton, V. (1969) Do Children Talk to their Parents. Mothers' Union
Whiting, J. W. M. (1960) Identification and Resource Mediation in
    Personality Development in Children (Ed) I. Iscoe and H. Stevenson.
    University of Texas Press
Wiener, R. S. P. (1970) Drugs and School Children. Longmans
Willmott, P. (1966) Adolescent Boys in East London. Routledge and Kegan
    Paul
Winnicott, D. W. (1965) The Family and Individual Development.
    Tavistock Publications
Wood, D. (1969) The Four Gospels. New Society, 18.12.69
Youth Service Development Council (1969) Youth and Community Work in
    the 70's. HMSO